far above
RUBIES

You're God's favorite!

♡ Blau

far above RUBIES

The Power and Promise of a Covenant-Keeping Woman

TAMARA
UZELAC HALL

Covenant Communications, Inc.

Cover painting: *One Little Light Left* © by Jen Tolman, www.jentolman.com
Interior Flowers © Olga Korneeva, Creative Market

Cover design by Christina Marcano © 2022 by Covenant Communications, Inc.

Published by Covenant Communications, Inc.
American Fork, Utah

Printed in the United States of America
First Printing: March 2022

29 28 27 26 25 24 23 22   10 9 8 7 6 5 4 3

ISBN-13: 978-1-52441-977-6

To Jim and our girls

משפחתי

Contents

ה Her Attributes—Verses 26–30

ו Her Reward—Verse 31

Proverbs 31:10–31

10 Who can find a virtuous woman? for her price is far above rubies.

11 The heart of her husband doth safely trust in her, so that he shall have no need of spoil.

12 She will do him good and not evil all the days of her life.

13 She seeketh wool, and flax, and worketh willingly with her hands.

14 She is like the merchants' ships; she bringeth her food from afar.

15 She riseth also while it is yet night, and giveth meat to her household, and a portion to her maidens.

16 She considereth a field, and buyeth it: with the fruit of her hands she planteth a vineyard.

17 She girdeth her loins with strength, and strengtheneth her arms.

18 She perceiveth that her merchandise is good: her candle goeth not out by night.

19 She layeth her hands to the spindle, and her hands hold the distaff.

20 She stretcheth out her hand to the poor; yea, she reacheth forth her hands to the needy.

21 She is not afraid of the snow for her household: for all her household are clothed with scarlet.

22 She maketh herself coverings of tapestry; her clothing is silk and purple.

23 Her husband is known in the gates, when he sitteth among the elders of the land.

24 She maketh fine linen, and selleth it; and delivereth girdles unto the merchant.

25 Strength and honour are her clothing; and she shall rejoice in time to come.

26 She openeth her mouth with wisdom; and in her tongue is the law of kindness.

27 She looketh well to the ways of her household, and eateth not the bread of idleness.

28 Her children arise up, and call her blessed; her husband also, and he praiseth her.

29 Many daughters have done virtuously, but thou excellest them all.

30 Favour is deceitful, and beauty is vain: but a woman that feareth the Lord, she shall be praised.

31 Give her of the fruit of her hands; and let her own works praise her in the gates.

אֵשֶׁת־חַיִל מִי יִמְצָא וְרָחֹק מִפְּנִינִים מִכְרָהּ: ¹⁰
בָּטַח בָּהּ לֵב בַּעְלָהּ וְשָׁלָל לֹא יֶחְסָר: ¹¹
גְּמָלַתְהוּ טוֹב וְלֹא־רָע כֹּל יְמֵי חַיֶּיהָ: ¹²
דָּרְשָׁה צֶמֶר וּפִשְׁתִּים וַתַּעַשׂ בְּחֵפֶץ כַּפֶּיהָ: ¹³
הָיְתָה כָּאֳנִיּוֹת סוֹחֵר מִמֶּרְחָק תָּבִיא לַחְמָהּ: ¹⁴
וַתָּקָם בְּעוֹד לַיְלָה וַתִּתֵּן טֶרֶף לְבֵיתָהּ וְחֹק לְנַעֲרֹתֶיהָ: ¹⁵
זָמְמָה שָׂדֶה וַתִּקָּחֵהוּ מִפְּרִי כַפֶּיהָ נָטְעָה כָּרֶם: ¹⁶
חָגְרָה בְעוֹז מָתְנֶיהָ וַתְּאַמֵּץ זְרוֹעֹתֶיהָ: ¹⁷
טָעֲמָה כִּי־טוֹב סַחְרָהּ לֹא־יִכְבֶּה בַלַּיְלָה נֵרָהּ: ¹⁸
יָדֶיהָ שִׁלְּחָה בַכִּישׁוֹר וְכַפֶּיהָ תָּמְכוּ פָלֶךְ: ¹⁹
כַּפָּהּ פָּרְשָׂה לֶעָנִי וְיָדֶיהָ שִׁלְּחָה לָאֶבְיוֹן: ²⁰
לֹא־תִירָא לְבֵיתָהּ מִשָּׁלֶג כִּי כָל־בֵּיתָהּ לָבֻשׁ שָׁנִים: ²¹
מַרְבַדִּים עָשְׂתָה־לָּהּ שֵׁשׁ וְאַרְגָּמָן לְבוּשָׁהּ: ²²
נוֹדָע בַּשְּׁעָרִים בַּעְלָהּ בְּשִׁבְתּוֹ עִם־זִקְנֵי־אָרֶץ: ²³
סָדִין עָשְׂתָה וַתִּמְכֹּר וַחֲגוֹר נָתְנָה לַכְּנַעֲנִי: ²⁴
עֹז־וְהָדָר לְבוּשָׁהּ וַתִּשְׂחַק לְיוֹם אַחֲרוֹן: ²⁵
פִּיהָ פָּתְחָה בְחָכְמָה וְתוֹרַת־חֶסֶד עַל־לְשׁוֹנָהּ: ²⁶
צוֹפִיָּה הֲלִיכוֹת בֵּיתָהּ וְלֶחֶם עַצְלוּת לֹא תֹאכֵל: ²⁷
קָמוּ בָנֶיהָ וַיְאַשְּׁרוּהָ בַּעְלָהּ וַיְהַלְלָהּ: ²⁸
רַבּוֹת בָּנוֹת עָשׂוּ חָיִל וְאַתְּ עָלִית עַל־כֻּלָּנָה: ²⁹
שֶׁקֶר הַחֵן וְהֶבֶל הַיֹּפִי אִשָּׁה יִרְאַת־יְהוָה הִיא תִתְהַלָּל: ³⁰
תְּנוּ־לָהּ מִפְּרִי יָדֶיהָ וִיהַלְלוּהָ בַשְּׁעָרִים מַעֲשֶׂיהָ: ³¹

Preface

AT THE OCTOBER 2020 GENERAL conference, our prophet, President Russell M. Nelson, expressed his desire to know more about the gathering of Israel. He told us that he had prayed, read, "feasted upon every related scripture," and asked the Lord to increase his understanding of the gathering. Then he shared this experience: "So imagine my delight when I was led recently to a new insight. With the help of two Hebrew scholars, I learned that one of the Hebraic meanings of the word *Israel* is 'let God prevail.'"[1] The prophet's process to gain this new knowledge and understanding about the gathering describes my own journey as I prayed about, read, and feasted on the proverb of a virtuous woman, found in Proverbs 31:10–31. I have spent the last six years studying Hebrew and have come to love this precious and precise language. Hebrew has changed the way I read and study my scriptures. Like President Nelson, I too have found that the Hebrew translation of a word can enhance, or even completely alter, my understanding of a scripture and at the same time strengthen my testimony.

That is exactly what it did when I read and studied the proverb of a virtuous woman in Hebrew.

After a careful study of the proverb, I have come to understand in a whole new way what it means to be virtuous. The proverb of a virtuous woman teaches us about our relationship with Jesus Christ, why keeping covenants is essential, and just how much our Heavenly Parents and Jesus love and trust us.

This book would not have been possible without the assistance of many incredible scholars. I would like to thank Hebrew scholars Carli Anderson, PhD; Geri Clements, MS; Mandella Green; and Corrinne R. Allen. I would also like to thank religious and secular scholars Margot J. Butler, EdM; Jenny Reeder, PhD; Janiece Johnson, PhD; Sharon Staples, PhD; Addie Fuhriman, PhD; Suzette Gee Kunz, PhD; Holly Butterfield Rawlings, MA; Thalene Fairbanks; Danene Torgesen; Rebecca Dowdle; Jamie Evans; Jenee Uzelac; Becky Farley; Holly Howarth; Susan Stanger; Sara Sargent; Alecia Williams; Laurel Christensen Day; Lisa Roper; Samantha Millburn; Laura Combrink; Carly M. Springer; Laura Muir; Charles Brown; Bliss Roberts; and the Book Club Babes of Iona, Idaho. And of course, I would like to thank all those who have allowed me to share their virtuous and beautiful stories.

Thou Art a Virtuous Woman

OKAY, SO LET'S TALK ABOUT the proverb of a virtuous woman. I think it is both amazing and overwhelming. Amazing because it is scripture about women, given by a woman. Overwhelming because for much of my life, I never felt like I measured up to those verses of scripture or ever would. When I was thirty-four years old and single, I was certain I was out of the running for being virtuous, because according to verse 11, the first qualifier is marriage. However, Hebrew changed all of that, and I am so excited to show you what I found. So, friends, grab your scriptures, and let's dig in!

The proverb is like a painting by Monet: "Viewed up close, the brushstrokes seem haphazard, but from a step or two away dots and splatters merge to become the cumulative image of a wise and valiant woman."[2] This proverb has been considered by some religious scholars to be a song, a heroic hymn, or an allegory.[3] As a song or hymn, it praises a virtuous woman, but when treated as an allegory, I believe that more profound meaning and significance is found within each verse.

By taking a look at the proverb of a virtuous woman allegorically and using the original Hebrew text, there is a possibility that, like the impressionistic painting metaphor, this proverb may be a "captivating and complex portrait—one that would be reclaimed, repainted, and renamed by sages for generations to come."[4] This book will zoom in on the individual brush strokes and then examine the whole image to find an inspiring and timely depiction of what being a virtuous woman really means.

Let's start with an up-close look at the literal translation of the proverb. At first glance, it seems to be a laundry list of "to-dos" for when you say, "I do." It defines a "virtuous" woman as one who is married; makes her husband happy; weaves the material that she will use to sew her clothing; gardens; owns a vineyard; cooks; is strong—*really* strong—;wakes up very early (or more than likely never goes to sleep); is charitable; helps the poor; has a well-known husband; is not afraid of the snow; dresses herself and her family very well; works outside the home to help bring in extra money; is kind and wise; is not idle; is loved, blessed, and praised by her children and husband; fears the Lord and . . . probably fears a nervous breakdown, too! It should really read, "Who can find a virtuous woman? Let me know, because she has probably passed out from utter exhaustion!" Lowell L. Bennion, a celebrated educator, shared his opinion on this proverb:

> It seems likely to me that this passage could
> have been written by a man who wanted to

be well provided for by a hard-working wife but who perhaps was less willing to expend the same effort himself. It also seems to me that this ancient ideal lacks any sense that women also need intellectual, social, and spiritual fulfillment. I am not sure, looking at the average congregation of Latter-day Saint mothers, that they need to be told to stay up later, get up earlier, or work harder than they are already doing.[5]

Can I get an amen?!

This proverb has taken on multiple meanings throughout history and can be read from many points of view. To mainstream Christianity, it is a biblical portrait of an ideal, heroic woman. For Jews, it serves as a reminder of a woman's value and honors her. I was fascinated to learn that in the Jewish faith a husband recites or sings "*Eshet Hayil*" ("Virtuous Woman") to his wife every Shabbat (Jewish Sabbath) for these very reasons. But what if the proverb goes beyond the literal meaning? In many instances, this proverb has been thought of as merely a "description of desirable virtues and capabilities of a good wife,"[6] portraying her as a "superwoman" in almost "superhuman" terms.[7] In reality, this proverb is not about an ideal woman but about Christ's people.

WOMEN AS A SYMBOL

In scripture, women are often used as a type or symbol for Christ's Church and His covenant people (see Matthew

25:1–13, Hosea 3, Isaiah 23, Revelation 12:1–7, 17).[8] The symbol of Christ as the Bridegroom and the Church as the bride is very prevalent throughout scripture. I believe that the proverb of a virtuous woman was not written to inundate women with responsibilities disproportionate to that of men but instead to wisely direct *all* of us, men and women, back to Him. For the purpose of this book, however, it will be addressed to women.

Now, here's where we dig into Proverbs 31:10–31. Let's see what it's all about.

The Structure

The first thing we have to do is take a look at the setup or structure of these twenty-two verses. In the Hebrew text, this proverb is a poem written in acrostic format.[9] You may remember writing an acrostic poem in elementary school. It's the style of poetry where you write your name (or a word) vertically down the side of the paper and then write a sentence or word that begins with each letter in the word. The acrostic style in the proverb doesn't spell out anything but instead lists all twenty-two letters of the Hebrew alphabet in order, making the proverb easier to memorize.

The proverb is attributed to the mother of King Lemuel, who is mentioned in Proverbs 31:1: "The words of king Lemuel, the prophecy that his mother taught him." She is advising him concerning a prospective bride. Traditional commentators have identified that this woman is actually Bathsheba speaking to her son Solomon and that "Lemuel" is a title meaning "one who belongs to God or is Dedicated to God."[10] Curiously, some scholars believe an anonymous author wrote the poem for devout Jews to easily memorize and repeat on a regular basis.[11] Whoever wrote it, one thing is certain: it is twenty-two verses of wise, biblical advice concerning the qualities that should be found in a virtuous woman.[12] As an allegory, it could even be wise advice from *the* Mother to *the* Son, "one who is dedicated to God," concerning the qualities He should look for in His people.

This poem, hymn, or allegory has a symbolic structure that will help us understand its overall meaning and purpose. Verses 10 and 31 are considered the bookends. Verse 10 asks, "Who can find a virtuous woman?" Verse 31 answers, "Give her of the fruit of her hands, and let her own works praise her in the gates." These two verses complement each other while also holding together twenty verses of instruction in between them. The twenty verses of instruction are grouped into four main sections, each with five verses.[13]

א Verse 10	Her worth
ב Verses 11–15	Herself and her household
ג Verses 16–20	Her labors
ד Verses 21–25	Her coverings
ה Verses 26–30	Her attributes
ו Verse 31	Her reward

Why five verses? Five is symbolic throughout scripture; it is a representation of God's grace and protection.[14] A few examples of this include:

- The first five books of the Old Testament, also called the Torah or the Pentateuch (Genesis, Exodus, Leviticus, Numbers, Deuteronomy).
- The Ten Commandments are broken into two quintets: the first five are about God and His relationship with mankind, and the second five are about mankind and his relationship with others.[15]
- The number five played an important role in the construction of Moses's tabernacle.[16]
- David chose five smooth stones from the brook to defeat Goliath (1 Samuel 17:40).
- Five loaves of bread fed five thousand (Matthew 14:13–21).

These examples show how the Lord uses the number five to teach and remind His people of His power, the protection He offers, and the grace He will give when they follow His word. The structure of the proverb of a virtuous woman follows a similar pattern.

Individually, the verses in Proverbs 31:10–31 may seem overwhelming, but when grouped into quintets, and using the Hebrew definitions rather than modern interpretation, the proverb perfectly demonstrates the Lord's power, protection, and grace over His people. It is a brilliantly written poem that can show how the Father feels about His daughters, sharing beautiful truths about who we are as women and why we are so important to Him. So deeply immersed in symbolism, this proverb may be a description of a wise and virtuous woman's personal relationship with her Savior and how she has become centered in Him.

This proverb is a call for every woman to reconsider and recognize her worth, understand the extraordinary role she is already playing in the world, and gain a knowledge of the rewards that await her.

NOTES

HER WORTH—VERSE 10

10.

Who can find a virtuous woman? for her price is far above rubies.

10. אֵשֶׁת־חַיִל מִי יִמְצָא וְרָחֹק מִפְּנִינִים מִכְרָהּ:

IN 1998, I WAS HIRED as a full-time seminary teacher in Salt Lake City, Utah. I can assure you that I was not hired for my scriptural intellect or spiritual prowess. I didn't even know that Christ came to America until I was in the Missionary Training Center (MTC). So when it was time to teach the Old Testament, you can imagine how utterly clueless I was. I studied hard and ended up having a lot of fun with the books of the Old Testament that year. But when I came to the book of Proverbs, specifically the proverb regarding a virtuous woman, I was baffled. Verse 10, the first verse of the proverb, had me stumped. I knew nothing about rubies. So, I decided to go to a reliable source—I called a local jeweler to find out just how much rubies were worth. Here's how our conversation went:

Me: "Umm, yes, I was wondering if you could tell me how much rubies cost?"

Jeweler: "Well, that depends on the size of the ruby and if it is real or manufactured."

Me: "Oh, OK. How about a real ruby about the size of a quarter?"

Jeweler: "The size of a quarter? There's no such thing. I've never seen a real ruby the size of a quarter."

Me: "All right then, how about the size of a nickel?"

Jeweler (choking on his response): "A nickel?"

Me: "Well, what size do rubies come in, then?"

Jeweler: "Ma'am, if you had a real ruby the size of a quarter, you and your entire family, and maybe your extended family, could retire because it would be worth so much."

Me: "Really? Hmmmm, then how about a real ruby the size of a dime?"

Jeweler: "Ma'am, do you know anything about rubies?"

He shared with me everything he knew about rubies, and at the end of our conversation he said, "Speaking of *real* rubies, I've never even seen one!"

That conversation changed everything for me, and it began my quest to really understand the proverb.

Who can find a virtuous woman?

This verse opens with a question or riddle: "Who can find?" It implies that finding a virtuous woman would be a miraculous event. Is a virtuous woman rare? Is she hard to find? When viewed as part of an allegory, verse 10 may not be pointing to an impossible superwoman. Instead, it may be highlighting what makes her virtuous, her true value, and who can afford her.

Today, we have unfortunately limited the word *virtuous* to refer only to modesty and chastity, but the term has a more significant value and meaning. In both Hebrew and Greek, virtue is defined as, "strength, power."[17] Alma the Younger understood this power as he served a mission among the Zoramites. He knew that the only way to convert the Zoramites was to "try the *virtue* of the word of God" (Alma 31:5; emphasis added). Alma didn't try the *modesty* of the word of God; he tried the *power* or *strength* of the word of God. Near the end of the Book of Mormon, Mormon describes to his son Moroni the deplorable state of the Nephites. He explains that many of the daughters of the Lamanites were taken prisoners and were deprived of "that which was most dear and precious above all things, which is chastity and virtue" (Moroni 9:9). These women were not only deprived of their chastity but also of their *power*.

Now, add the suffix -*ous* which means, "possessing or full of a given quality," and we can see that a *virtuous* woman possesses or is filled with strength or power. This virtue, power, or strength that a virtuous woman has will determine **_her price_**.

for her price is far above rubies

Since the proverb is given by a mother to her son and is about choosing a bride, then *her price* is a bride price or a *mohar*.[18] A mohar is the bridegroom's price that he pays to the bride's father for her hand in marriage prior to getting married, and it seals or acts as a covenant between the two. The mohar was often decided upon based on the wealth or standing of the bride. In eastern countries, the bride price would usually be paid in gold, silver, or precious things such as jewelry or gems. A biblical example of this is found in the engagement of Rebekah to Isaac: "And the servant brought forth jewels of silver, and jewels of gold, and raiment, and gave them to Rebekah: he gave also to her brother and to her mother precious things" (Genesis 24:53). Sometimes the bride price can be a service rendered, as in the case with Jacob for Rachel (see Genesis 29:18); deeds of valor might also be accepted in place of a dowry (Joshua 15:16, 1 Samuel 18:25).[19] The bride price of the virtuous woman has been predetermined, based on the power and strength that the woman will bring to the marriage. That price *is far above rubies*.

The jeweler did a great job of educating me on the value of rubies; they're worth a lot of moolah. Learning this gave me great insight into the price of a virtuous woman being *far beyond rubies*. But learning about the word *rubies* in Hebrew changed everything. *Rubies* in this verse is *peninim* and means "corals or pearls."[20] While mentioned only a few dozen times in scripture, pearls are the biblical standard for excellence and beauty, worth far more than rubies. It is believed that pearls were considered among the most precious of gems in the ancient world.[21] Pearls were seen as very precious in New Testament times (Matthew 13:45–46; 1 Timothy 2:9), so precious, in fact, that the Lord implemented them in His design for the city of New Jerusalem (Revelation 18:16, 21:21).[22] Verse 10 of this proverb might more appropriately read, "Who can find a woman filled with power? for she is invaluable." Comparing the virtuous woman to pearls shows she is "truly priceless. Money cannot buy her; she is off the scale of monetary value."[23]

After learning the worth of "rubies," I immediately wondered, *Wow! Then who in the world could even afford a virtuous woman?* Well, miraculously, though symbolically, there is a Bridegroom that will pay this extreme and seemingly exorbitant price to the Father for His bride, and He is the only One who could truly afford to—the Savior, Jesus Christ.

NOTES

HERSELF AND HER
HOUSEHOLD—VERSES 11–15

11.

The heart of her husband doth safely trust in her, so that he shall have no need of spoil.

11. בָּטַח בָּהּ לֵב בַּעְלָהּ וְשָׁלָל לֹא יֶחְסָר׃

I WAS THIRTY YEARS OLD and very single the first time I taught the seminary lesson on this proverb. The title of the lesson was "Proverbs 31:10–31: We Should Marry Someone Who has Christlike Characteristics."[24] After reading verse 11, I remember thinking, "Someday I will be virtuous . . . someday." I thought this verse was saying that the first qualifier for being virtuous was having a husband, and I didn't come close to qualifying—I had never even had a boyfriend. I thought, *If the family is central to Heavenly Father's plan of happiness, then apparently, I am way off-center.* Thankfully, the Hebrew text allows us to explore the possibility that this verse isn't referring to wedding invitations or registering for gifts. Instead, verse 11 is symbolic of a woman's covenant relationship with Christ, which *every* woman can have regardless of her marital status.

The heart of her husband

In the Bible, the most commonly used Hebrew word for husband is *ish* and means man or husband, but the word used in this verse is *baal* and can be translated as "owner," "Lord," or "master."[25] So, another way to read verse 11 would be, "The heart of her Lord/Master doth safely trust in her." Allegorically, the use of *baal* could be intentional, guiding us to the true identity of the husband. The only Lord or Master who owns any of us is the Savior Jesus Christ. In this verse, Christ is the husband. He has asked the virtuous woman for her hand in marriage, meaning He has invited her to make covenants with Him.

Throughout scripture, the Savior is referred to as the "husband" or "bridegroom" (Isaiah 54:5, 62:5; Matthew 25:1–13; Revelation 19:7–9; D&C 33:17; 133:10,19). In an *Ensign* article titled "The Marriage Metaphor," author Richard K. Hart points out that "more commonly, the Lord referred to himself as a Bridegroom or Husband of the house of Israel: 'For thy Maker is thine husband; the Lord of hosts is his name' (Isaiah 54:5); 'For I am married unto you' (Jeremiah 3:14); 'I was an husband unto them' (Jeremiah 31:32)."[26] "The description of Christ as the Bridegroom and Israel (us) as the bride is among the most commonly used metaphors in scripture" because it was something that most people could understand and relate to.[27] The marriage metaphor is used symbolically to help us understand that the covenants we make with the Savior and the relationship we have with Him are like the relationship between a real husband and wife.[28] In a marriage, there is a mutual promise of love, loyalty, and fidelity, and the same is true for the covenantal relationship we make with the Savior.[29] The moment we enter into any covenant with Christ, we symbolically become His wife, and He becomes our husband. He is married to the covenant people, and He takes the symbolic title of Husband.[30]

The bride price has been agreed upon and paid to the Father. The Apostle Paul teaches us, "For ye are bought with a price" (1 Corinthians 6:20), and Peter tells us that we have been redeemed, but not with "corruptible things, as silver and gold . . . But with the precious blood of Christ" (1 Peter 1:18–19). Now, going back to the virtuous woman's price being far above pearls, consider the Savior's parable in Matthew 13:45–46: "Again, the kingdom of heaven is like unto a merchant man, seeking goodly pearls: Who, when he had found one pearl of great price, went and sold all that he had, and bought it." This verse is commonly used to describe the treasures of the gospel or Church membership. However, it may now be interpreted to mean that the merchant man represents Christ, and the virtuous woman is like the goodly *pearl*. She is His *pearl of great price*. And Christ was willing to sell all that He had . . . even His own life. He bought the virtuous woman with the price of His own blood.

No matter what a woman's actual marital status is—single, married, widowed, or divorced—the moment she chooses to enter into a covenant relationship with Christ, she is married to Him, and through her covenants she becomes virtuous; she is filled with His power, His priesthood power. Nephi saw this in his vision of Christ's people: "And it came to pass that I, Nephi, beheld the power of the Lamb of God, that it descended upon the saints of the church of the Lamb, and upon the covenant people of the Lord . . . and they were armed with righteousness and with the power of God in great glory" (1 Nephi 14:14). Regarding this specific power in our daily lives, Elder D. Todd Christofferson taught that the source of moral and spiritual power is God. He then said, "Our access to that power is through our covenants with Him."[31] A perfect example of this covenant relationship in connection to the word *virtuous* and marriage is found in the book of Ruth.

Ruth is the only woman in scripture to be called "virtuous," and she was single (widowed) at the time (Ruth 3:11). Ruth was from Moab and did not belong to the house of Israel. She was not raised as a covenant-keeping woman. She married an Israelite husband, but after ten years of marriage, she became a widow. She had the choice to return and live with her family in Moab or to follow her mother-in-law, Naomi, back to Bethlehem, which was her husband's birthplace. She chose to follow Naomi, and her heartfelt vow is recorded in Ruth 1:16–17:

> And Ruth said, Entreat me not to leave thee, or to return from following after thee: for whither thou goest, I will go; and where thou lodgest, I will lodge: thy people shall be my people, and thy God my God:
>
> Where thou diest, will I die, and there will I be buried: the Lord do so to me, and more also, if ought but death part thee and me.

Ruth eventually meets a man named Boaz, and through what appears to be a divinely designed set of circumstances, she requests his hand in marriage. In answer to her request, Boaz says, "And now, my daughter, fear not; I will do to thee all that thou requirest: for all the city of my people doth know that thou art a *virtuous woman*" (Ruth 3:11; emphasis added). Ruth's commitment to Christ is what made her virtuous. That's it. Boaz's praise of her is solely conditional on the relationship she had with her God. Ruth ends up marrying Boaz, and it is from this union and their lineage that Jesus Christ will eventually come (see Matthew 1:5–6, 16).

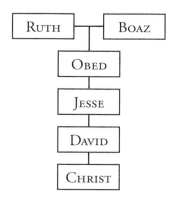

Many generations pass between David and Christ

As a single woman, Ruth was virtuous. It was her conversion and covenantal commitment to the God of Israel—"and thy God my God" (Ruth 1:16)—that made her virtuous, that filled her with spiritual strength and power. Ruth became married to Christ through the covenants she made.

For us today, the invitation to make covenants begins at the age of eight. The *moment* a young girl comes out of the waters of baptism, she is virtuous. Not because her vast array of sins have been washed away. Mormon taught that little children are not capable of sin, nor are they in need of repentance (see Moroni 8:9–14, 19).[32] The accurate and powerful message of baptism is that we have entered into our first priesthood covenant with the Savior, our Lord and Master. Elder Christofferson pointed this out when he said, "Our foundational covenant, the one in which we first pledge our willingness to take upon us the name of Christ, is confirmed by the ordinance of baptism . . . By this ordinance, we become part of the covenant people of the Lord."[33] On a young girl's baptism day, she covenants with God, and in doing so, becomes virtuous. She is immediately filled with His strength and His power. In her April 2020 general conference address, Sister Joy D. Jones shared that she did not know this truth when she was young: "My personal admission today is that as a woman I didn't realize, earlier in my life, that *I* had access, through my covenants, to the power of the priesthood."[34]

Can you imagine the positive effect it would have on our young women if they were taught and believed that from the time they are young girls they are filled with God's power, His priesthood power, and that they are already virtuous? That being virtuous has everything to do with her personal relationship with Christ and nothing to do with what she is wearing? President Russell M. Nelson taught that when our greatest desire is to let God prevail in our lives, "so many decisions become easier. So many issues become nonissues! You know how best to groom yourself."[35] Knowing that being virtuous means having a personal relationship with Christ will change behaviors and conversations. BYU professor and author Barbara Morgan Gardner powerfully pointed this out when she wrote, "Imagine what a difference it would make in the world if women of the Church truly understood their priesthood privileges and led their families and other women of the world using righteous principles and the power received through making and keeping sacred covenants."[36] This is the doctrine of Christ that our girls so desperately need, and it is a doctrine crucial to the value of all women. This knowledge and covenantal commitment are why the Savior can *safely trust in her so that he shall have no need of spoil.*

doth safely trust in her so that he shall have no need of spoil

Because He can safely trust in her, the Master will *have no need of spoil.* The symbolic meaning of this phrase is remarkable. The word *spoil* is associated with war, and there are plenty of Old Testament references to spoils of war.[37] After a war was won, the victors would take what was left from the city or people they destroyed: food, animals, booty or treasure, and even people whom they would enslave—all of which were referred to as the "spoils of war." These spoils were often in excess of what the victors already possessed. Going back to the proverb, why would the Lord *have no need of spoil*, or no need of excess or gain? Because a virtuous woman, a covenant-keeping woman, is *enough.*

As a virtuous woman, you are valued, and you are enough of everything for Him. You are spiritual enough, good enough, worthy enough, pretty enough, smart enough, thin enough, kind enough, a good enough mom, a good enough wife, a good enough daughter, and whatever enough you may feel you aren't. Oh, how I would have benefitted from knowing this at a young age. I have countless journal entries from when I was between the ages of ten and thirty-four where I questioned my worth because I thought I wasn't enough. So much of my worth was rooted in trying to be more or weigh less. For years, I had tethered my self-worth to marriage, bound by the number of dates or boyfriends I had, or the lack thereof.

No wonder I felt inadequate to teach this lesson to my seminary students! I had always assumed that this verse was just one more piece of evidence that I wasn't enough and that the rest of this proverb was God's way of making sure I knew that I would never measure up. But God is using verse 11 of this proverb to say—with exclamation points—that a covenant-keeping woman is enough!!! He teaches us that the covenant relationship that we have with the Savior is all He needs from us.

When women recognize that they are enough, are trusted, and have the Lord's power, they become emboldened to do His work. However, Satan spends so much of his time keeping us chained up in the idea that, more often than not, we fall short of this power and trust and will never be enough. His goal is to weaken us and prevent us from doing what we have been sent here to do—namely, the Lord's work. President Russell M. Nelson wants us to know this and said:

Most certainly, the adversary does not want you to understand the covenant you made at baptism or the profound endowment of knowledge and power you have received or will receive in the temple—the house of the Lord. And Satan certainly does not want you to understand that every time you worthily serve and worship in the temple, you leave armed with God's power and with His angels having "charge over" you. Satan and his minions will constantly contrive roadblocks to prevent you from understanding the spiritual gifts with which you have been and can be blessed.[38]

Jesus Christ is confident in our abilities and trusts us to further His work in whatever capacity He may require of us. As virtuous women filled with His power, we can do and are doing amazing things. In our covenant relationship with Christ lies mutual respect, loyalty, trust, and love—of course that's enough. He has need of nothing else, and as a result, we have the power to do Him good and not evil all the days of our lives.

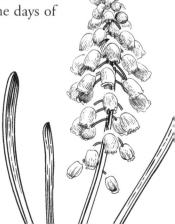

N O T E S

12.

She will do him good and not evil all the days of her life.

12. גְּמָלַתְהוּ טוֹב וְלֹא־רָע כֹּל יְמֵי חַיֶּיהָ:

I WAS NINE YEARS OLD when I wrote the following journal entry in answer to my second-grade teacher's writing prompt for the day:

October 3, 1980

Think about your own secret place and tell us about it.

> *T.V. Room. First I go up the stairs then I turn then I go strate then I am there. Well it has a chair and a couch and most of all a t.v. It has a book shelf and a fire place and a desk with a tele-phone. I either read watch t.v. or I rest or I do my home work or I play like I am a movie star and I sing. No one comes whith me becuse I mostly like being alone. I like being alone when I get in lots of trouble and start to cry. I realy like my secret place a lot. why? to be alone and cry and so I don't get in any trouble any more. The end.*

This entry makes it sound like I was a mischievous, disobedient child who was always getting into trouble . . . and liked singing. But here's the thing, I was a pretty obedient child. When I was a little girl, the worst form of punishment—I mean the *worst*—was the thought of disappointing my parents. You could spank me, ground me, take away a privilege . . . MEH. But if I heard the slightest hint of "we are so disappointed in you" from my parents, my world collapsed. I'm the oldest child, and I'm a pleaser. Doing good all the days of my life was the only aspiration I had . . . and is something I am still striving to do. But is doing good all the days of my life even possible?

Verses 10 and 11 have helped us understand who we are and realize that we are enough. But how much of *enough* do we need to be? Is *enough* equivalent to perfection? Traditionally verse 12 has been understood to mean that a woman repays her husband financially with goodness and that she will do him good throughout the duration of her life with him.[39] However, we have learned from verses 10 and 11 that because a woman is filled with power, believes that she is enough, and is trusted, she will naturally be a powerful benefit to Christ, and not in a monetary way at all. This relationship of trust with the Husband is the driving force to doing *Him good and not evil all the days of her life.*

She will do him good and not evil

The first word of this verse is גָּמַל (*gamal*) and means "to deal fully, or to deal bountifully with."[40] The virtuous woman *will do him good*, or she will deal bountifully with Christ. The abundant goodness spoken of in this verse is not about a financial contribution. The *good* that we perform has everything to do with faith.

In Hebrew, the word for faith is אֱמוּנָה (*emunah*), which means, "to be firm and steadfast." Its root is *Aman*, meaning "to support." In English, when we talk about our faith, we most often say, "I have faith in God," placing the action on Him and hoping He will act on our behalf. But the word *emunah* actually places the responsibility and action on us, the ones who "firmly support God."

A great example of this is found in the battle scene from Exodus 17. Israel was fighting against Amalek and his people, and Israel was facing imminent defeat. Moses, Aaron, and Hur went up to the top of a hill. When Moses held up his hands, Israel prevailed, but when he let his hands fall down, Amalek prevailed (Exodus 17:10–11), "But Moses' hands grew weary; so they took a stone and put it under him, and he sat upon it, and Aaron and Hur held up his hands, one on one side, and the other on the other side; so his hands were steady [emunah] until the going down of the sun" (Exodus 17:12). It was the firm and steadfast support of Aaron and Hur, who held Moses's arms, not the support of Moses, that allowed Israel to win the battle.[41]

When we hear or say, "I have faith in God," maybe we could think about it this way: "I will do what I can to firmly support God." James taught that faith without works is dead, and so doing what God asks is what gives us our faith in Him

(James 2:14–26). When we are exercising our faith by keeping our covenants and commandments, we are doing Him good.

Now, there may be some covenants or commandments that we don't completely understand or that to the world may seem outdated or unpopular. There may even be some that we genuinely struggle with and, as a result, we have given up all hope, ready to throw in the towel and disqualify ourselves from the celestial kingdom.

Many years ago, while attending BYU, I had enrolled in a Doctrine and Covenants class taught by Dr. Susan Easton Black that changed the way I view my struggles with faith and doing good. It was a semester I will never forget; I was fed spiritual truths and insights that changed my relationship with my Savior.

One specific example of this was the day she taught me the importance of keeping my covenants and the Savior's role in my ability (or lack thereof) to do it well enough. She asked us to consider the first covenants we made with the Savior: our baptismal covenants. She then asked the class to consider how we would answer the following questions: "Are you mourning with those that mourn? Are you comforting those who stand in need of comfort? Are you standing as a witness of God at all times and in all things, and in all places that ye may be in, even until death? Were you able to answer 'I am' to any of those questions? *I am* mourning with those who mourn, or at least *I am* trying?" She then taught that the answer, *I Am* in Hebrew, is Jehovah's name. It is the name the Savior gave in the Old Testament when He introduced Himself to Moses on Mount Sinai: "I AM THAT I AM" (Exodus 3:14). Dr. Black pointed out that when we answer in His name, I Am, we acknowledge that we may not be perfect at keeping our covenants but that through His enabling power, we can.[42]

Now, to take this idea one step further, the words "I Am That I Am" also translate in Hebrew as "I Will Become Who I Will Become."[43] When it comes to falling short of being a perfect covenant keeper, we must remember that the Great I Am will perfect us, strengthen us, and help us become who we are to become if we let Him. The word *perfect* in Hebrew and Greek both translate as "complete, having reached its end." The Husband, who is a completely whole, finished, resurrected being, trusts that we are trying. He knows that we are not perfect yet, that we haven't reached our end. He has confidence that we are becoming who we were sent here to become. He cares more about the direction we are going than where we have been, and "to Him our direction is more important than our speed."[44] Standing on our individual covenant path is always the right direction—and trying our best to keep those covenants is what doing Him good and not *evil* is all about.

The word for *evil* in this proverb is רע (*ra*), which means "injury, harm, ethically bad or wicked."[45] A covenant-keeping woman doesn't have the disposition to do her husband harm. She is not ethically bad. Will she mess up? Yes. Is she going to sin? Sure. But her faith in Christ keeps her moving along the covenant path, one that is uniquely her own. Her emunah helps her to do what she can to support Him steadfastly. John

Gill, a sixteenth-century biblical scholar who recognized that the husband of the parable is Christ, eloquently summed up what verse 12 says about the virtuous woman when he said, "She will repay good unto him, give him thanks for all the good things bestowed by him on her; will seek his interest, and promote his honour and glory to the uttermost; all the good works she does, which she is qualified for, and ready to perform, are all done in his name and strength, and with a view to his glory."[46] A virtuous woman will continue with this pattern of doing good, through her faith, *all the days of her life*.

all the days of her life

*Day*s means the length of one's life.[47] We could interpret the phrase *all the days of her life* to mean that we are to carefully measure our days on an obscure scale of decency, hopefully doing enough good and not evil from the moment we wake up, then resting our weary minds and trying to fall asleep each night. But perhaps a better interpretation of this phrase is that the total of all the virtuous woman's acts throughout the length of her lifetime were good.

How many of us need to cut ourselves a break? Nine-year-old me sure did. We would all benefit from knowing that we are I AM and are becoming who we were sent to become, and that the steps we take in life, good and bad, mischievous and obedient, are all essential to building our emunah. And our emunah, throughout our lifetime, will be good enough.

NOTES

13.

She seeketh wool, and flax, and worketh willingly with her hands.

13. דָּרְשָׁה צֶמֶר וּפִשְׁתִּים וַתַּעַשׂ בְּחֵפֶץ כַּפֶּיהָ:

Now, THIS VERSE HAD ME stumped. I'm not even kidding. When I taught the virtuous woman lesson, I would casually skip over this verse. Not because I didn't understand it . . . but because I did. I mean, how in the world could I teach my twenty-first century Gen Z students that God expected women to grow flax, shear their sheep, and willingly work with their own hands—with no help from anyone? Thankfully, knowing the context of this verse saves all of us from this ancient approach to becoming virtuous. So, if you are not in the business of gardening, farming, or raising livestock, there is hope. This verse could be echoing Sister Elaine L. Jack's encouraging words to the women of the Church: "To be a woman of covenant is a sacred and holy responsibility. It is uniquely ours. It is not by chance that we are on the Lord's errand at this time."[48] Wool and flax are symbols of the "Lord's errand," and verse 13 now delves into and defines the specific and symbolic type of good that the virtuous woman chooses to do for her husband.

She seeketh

The first word of this verse is *seek* or דרשׁ (*deresh*). This word can be used to describe the process of not only seeking, but "inquiring of, seeking deity in prayer and worship."[49] The idea that the virtuous woman is *seeking deity in prayer and worship* as she begins His work is a testament to her doing Him good. It is a testament to the life she has chosen, the sacred work in which she will engage. But the text says she seeks *wool* and *flax*, not the Lord. What does that mean? These two textiles are symbolic, and to understand the specific good the virtuous woman is going to do, we need to know what they represent. To the covenant Israelite, these two textiles hold deep symbolism and take on additional meanings.

wool

Wool was a common, durable cloth, and it was worn as an everyday fabric by most people. However, wool is more than lamb's hair spun into yarn. As a symbol, it "points to the need for the Atonement of Jesus, 'the *Lamb* of God, which taketh away the sins of the world' (John 1:29)."[50] Isaiah wrote, "Come now, and let us reason together, saith the Lord: though your sins be as scarlet, they shall be as white as snow; though they be red like crimson, they shall be as wool" (Isaiah 1:18). To the covenant Israelite, wool represented what the Atonement of Jesus Christ can do for the natural man. It was an emblem of physical life, sin, the need for a Savior, and salvation from physical death.

and flax

Flax is the plant that gives us linen. The plant produces strong cellulose fibers inside the stalk that are used to make the linen, with adorable tiny blue flowers that adorn the top of each stalk. Unlike wool, linen was rarely worn as an everyday fabric. It was mainly associated with the sacred clothing of the priesthood, the holy tabernacle, and temple accessories. In the New Testament, linen is associated with heavenly beings and God.[51] The book of Revelation describes Christ's people as being "arrayed in fine linen" when He returns (Revelation 15:6). They are pictured as the virtuous woman, the bride: "And to her [the covenant bride] was granted that she should be arrayed in fine linen, clean and white: for the fine linen is the *righteousness of saints*" (Revelation 19:8; emphasis added).[52] To the covenant Israelite, linen represented righteousness; it was an emblem of spiritual life, holiness, and redemption from spiritual death.

As the children of Israel observed the law of Moses, they were forbidden from planting, growing, or mixing certain materials as a reminder of their covenants. Interestingly, wool and linen were not allowed to be mixed, nor were the two worn together. "What was the purpose of such performances? To remind them of their covenants. When they sowed a field, they were always reminded that Israel was a part of the covenant people, and they were not to intermingle with nations outside the covenant. That simple reminder was intended to remind them of their covenants."[53]

Only priests were allowed to mix the two materials (Leviticus 19:19, Deuteronomy 22:11).[54] While the priests performed temple rituals, their wool clothing symbolized physical life and the power that Christ's Atonement has to redeem mankind from sin and physical death. Their linen clothing symbolized spiritual life and the power that Christ's Atonement has to redeem mankind from the effects of sin and spiritual death. By seeking wool and flax, the virtuous woman understands that "man is a dual being, spiritual and physical" and like the priest, she tends to the physical and spiritual needs of mankind.[55]

and worketh willingly with her hands

After seeking and finding wool and flax, the virtuous woman *worketh willingly with her hands*. The word *willingly* means "delighting in, having pleasure in."[56] So, with pleasure and delight, she works with her hands for the Lord. Throughout this proverb, the word *hands* is used regularly. In Hebrew, a hand or palm is a symbol of power.[57] We delight in using our hands for the physical and spiritual good of Heavenly Father's children. Now, I have to admit something. This concept of "having pleasure in" caring for the spiritual and physical needs of others did not come easily for me until my mission.

When I turned twenty-one, I decided to serve a mission. In preparation, I was sent a list of items that I needed to purchase: skirts, nice blouses, comfortable shoes, a warm coat for winter, and more skirts. After a few days of shopping, I was able to get everything I needed except for a warm coat. It took several more shopping trips until, at last, I walked into a department store where I saw the most beautiful coat that I had ever seen. There it hung: a long, full-length, cream-colored wool coat with pearl buttons. I had to have it; I knew it was the one for me. We bought it, and it became my prized possession. I loved that coat so much. I entered the Missionary Training Center armed with my gorgeous coat . . . and maybe a testimony.

It was December, and I wore that coat every day in the MTC and then on the plane ride to my mission. My coat and I graciously stepped off the plane, ready to convert all of Fresno, California. I was picked up by the assistants to the president and taken to the mission office, where I was greeted by my first companion and trainer, Sister Gee. We loaded up our car with my luggage and immediately set off to teach an investigator. We pulled into a run-down part of town, and I was sure we were in the wrong place. I looked around, trying to figure out what we were doing there. Sister Gee parked and got out of the car, and I reluctantly followed. We walked up to the door of a small trailer, the kind that you pull behind a truck when you are camping, and knocked. The door flew open, and we were greeted by Angie, her boyfriend, and their four children. She invited us in. I could not believe that one person, much less a whole family, lived inside that trailer. We walked in, and my nostrils were assaulted by what smelled like day-old pork chop grease and stale cigarette smoke.

I cautiously stepped into the trailer and onto the dingy, tattered, and worn-out rug. I conspicuously looked that trailer up and down as Sister Gee made introductions. We were invited to sit down, and after taking one look at the very soiled couch, I thought, "There is no way I am sitting on that! My coat will get filthy!" My companion sat down without hesitation. I, however, paused for a moment and then cautiously sat down, but just on the edge of the couch so I wouldn't ruin my coat. Suddenly two of her kids ran over to me and tried to sit on my lap. They were so dirty. I was pretty sure they hadn't showered in months. You could actually see dirt embedded in their hands and faces. Worried about what they might do to my coat, I politely told the kids no and sat them down at my feet on the filthy floor.

Sister Gee began the visit with a prayer. Almost instinctively, their dog came over to me and jumped up, flopping its front paws onto my coat. I twitched and then watched those paws slowly, very slowly slide down my beautiful coat, leaving behind streaks of dirt (and who knows what else). After the prayer, Sister Gee began teaching the first lesson, but I didn't hear a word she said. I couldn't hear anything over the screaming tantrum I was having in my head about the stains on my coat. Waking me from my mental outburst, Sister Gee called my name and turned the rest of the lesson over to me. I was quite taken aback. I quickly gathered my thoughts, trying to recall what I had spent the last few weeks learning at the MTC. With trepidation and a lingering concern for my coat, I began to teach Angie and her family. I taught the lesson, shared a few scriptures, and bore my testimony. As I did this, something happened. I began to feel love for these people whom I had only known for twenty minutes. I saw Angie and her family as precious, valued daughters and sons of God.

Sister Gee jumped in and asked Angie if she believed that what we were teaching was true. Angie said that she did, and then my companion asked her if she would like to be baptized. *WAIT!* I thought. *You don't ask that question until we have met a few more times!* I wondered what in the world she was doing! I looked at my companion and back at Angie. My heart was pounding. What was she going to say? What if she said no? What were we supposed to do? I said a quick little prayer for Angie, hoping that she would accept the invitation to get baptized. Angie looked at us and said "Yeah, I would like that." I was bursting inside! She said yes!

My soul was saturated with joy. We finished up the lesson and said the closing prayer. Before I knew it, all of us were in one massive, loving embrace! All I cared about was this sweet woman and her family. The only thing that mattered to me was them. What I thought I loved changed to what the Lord loved. I had complete and overwhelming admiration and concern for Angie and each member of her family . . . including the dog. I walked out of that trailer with a changed heart. I could not stop smiling. I got into the car, and as we drove, the thought came, "You need to send the coat home." And so I did. The very next day, I boxed it up and drove it to the post office. Shedding the weight of that wool coat allowed me to delightfully seek after and share the true *wool and flax* with the people of California.

How wonderful that today, women ages fourteen and older can delight in doing the Lord good by caring for the physical and spiritual needs of others through ministering. In a letter to members of the Church, the First Presidency instructed, "Ministering is Christlike caring for others and helping meet their spiritual and temporal needs."[58] The Relief Society and Young Women have the opportunity to serve and be served together. Sister Jean B. Bingham, Relief Society General President, explained, "As we accept the opportunity to wholeheartedly minister to our sisters and brothers, we are blessed to become more spiritually refined, more in tune with the will of God, and more able to understand His plan to help each one return to Him."[59] President Russell M. Nelson spoke of the important role that a virtuous woman plays in the physical and spiritual needs of others:

> Today, let me add that we need women who know how to make important things happen by their faith and who are courageous defenders of morality and families in a sin-sick world. We need women who are devoted to shepherding God's children along the covenant path toward exaltation; women who know how to receive personal revelation, who understand the power and peace of the temple endowment; women who know how to call upon the powers of heaven to protect and strengthen children and families; women who teach fearlessly.[60]

Because of the love that we have for the Savior, we are engaged in the work of salvation with Him. As President Gordon B. Hinckley taught, "How magnificent will be the future as the Almighty rolls on His glorious work . . . through the selfless [service] of those whose hearts are filled with love for the Redeemer of the world."[61] A virtuous woman willingly assists in this work.

NOTES

14.

She is like the merchants' ships; she bringeth her food from afar.

14. הָיְתָה כָּאֳנִיּוֹת סוֹחֵר מִמֶּרְחָק תָּבִיא לַחְמָהּ׃

I HAVE A CONFESSION TO make. When I was first married, I subscribed to a few fancy cooking magazines. Not because I couldn't cook but because I wanted to be the best. The. Best. Cook. Ever. OK, so my confession isn't wanting to be the best cook ever, my confession is the reason: Michelle. Michelle is my husband's first wife, who passed away from breast cancer. When I got married, I stepped into shoes that I was made acutely aware I would never be able to fill. Nothing was ever said to me directly, but she was talked about and praised by everyone who knew her. I totally get that this is natural and normal, but my naive, jealous, insecure heart couldn't take it. Michelle was amazing, funny, friendly, loving, educated, spiritual, organized, clean, and pretty much perfect. However, the one thing she couldn't do was cook. Her cooking skills were the only thing *not* listed on her résumé of perfection. I immediately seized the opportunity to be better than her at something. Verse 14 was totally for me, or so I thought.

Thankfully, this verse goes beyond fancy cooking magazines. We can take heart and breathe a sigh of relief because the symbolic meaning behind the word *food* allows us to focus on the Savior instead of a savory dish. The "food" the virtuous woman brings from "afar" is like the food President Gordon B. Hinckley spoke of when he said, "There is hunger in the land, and a genuine thirst—a great hunger for the word of the Lord and an unsatisfied thirst for things of the Spirit. I am satisfied that the world is starved for spiritual food. Ours is the obligation and the opportunity to nourish the soul."[62] A virtuous woman will use *her food* to do just that.

She is like the merchants' ships; she bringeth her food

This simile "She is like the merchants' ships" would strike fear into the heart of anyone during biblical times because it implies a dangerous and arduous journey. The Hebrews were not a seafaring people and usually regarded the waters with vague terror.[63] This phrase is used to show us that the virtuous woman is doing something challenging that requires a great deal of effort and bravery. Besides an eclair, what food is so valuable that a woman would expend so much effort and grit to get it? Well, the Hebrew word for *food* in this verse is לֶחֶם (*lechem*) and means "bread" (I know, mmmm, bread).[64] But it is what bread often symbolizes in scripture that makes this so interesting. In Genesis 3:17–19, we are taught that as a result of the fall, Adam and Eve would have to rely on lechem to survive, "In the sweat of thy face shalt thou eat bread, till thou return unto the ground." The reference to bread in this verse is about Jesus Christ. Sure, Adam and Eve needed lechem to survive physically, but they would need *the* lechem to survive spiritually. The Savior taught,

"For the bread of God is he which cometh down from heaven, and giveth life unto the world. . . . I am the bread of life: he that cometh to me shall never hunger; and he that believeth on me shall never thirst" (John 6:33–35, 48). I believe that the author of this proverb is trying to teach us a powerful lesson about the food a woman is willing to go to great lengths to obtain. The virtuous woman's food is the *bread of life*. It is her testimony of Jesus Christ, and she went *afar* to obtain it.

from afar

Bringing her food or testimony *from afar* tells us of the great lengths the virtuous woman goes to obtain it. *Afar* means "a distant or remote place."[65] How far did she go to obtain her testimony? How far has she traveled? How far is she willing to keep going to obtain her testimony and, as this verse shows, to bring it back for others? Like a merchant's ship, her journey is bound to be met with a few storms. What do her personal storms look like? Does she walk to the edge of her faith and stand on the cliff of disbelief? What does she believe even amidst her uncertainties? Has she been swallowed up in grief to the point of absolute exhaustion? Has she experienced the engulfing abyss of sorrow or depression and called out in her suffering for the succoring power of the Savior's Atonement to save her? Will her tear-stained pillow stand as a witness of her turmoil? My pillow sure did. One specific spiritual journey of my own took me beyond what I would call distant or remote. It took me to a place that I had never imagined going, my crisis of faith.

I can vividly recall the day my mission companion and I were asked what we believed about Joseph Smith. I was sitting on a couch, and the sun was shining in through Levolor blinds hanging on the window. For the life of me, I can't remember what I said. I only remember the following thoughts immediately popping into my head: *You don't have a testimony of Joseph Smith. Did he really see what he said he saw? Maybe he was a fraud . . . like you . . . because you don't really know.* This thought struck me because I had never before questioned if Joseph Smith was a prophet of God or if he really had a vision. So, I decided to get an answer. I studied Joseph Smith—History and then decided to have my own James 1:5 experience. I did lack faith, and I needed to know. I got on my knees that night and asked. And waited. And waited. Nothing came, so I went to bed. I woke up that next morning, put on a skirt, and got back to work. I didn't get the "First Vision" answer I was hoping for, so I let it go and assumed Joseph Smith really was a prophet, figuring maybe I would get an answer one day.

Ten years later, during the summer of 2002, as I was preparing to teach the Doctrine and Covenants and Church History for the school year, one of my colleagues gave me an old 1980s Church history book and recommended that I read it. Now, one of the best things about being a full-time seminary teacher is *summer*! I would spend my summers reading, learning, attending seminars, reading some more, and preparing for the upcoming school year. That summer, I spent many weeks reading and poring over Church history books, so this recommendation seemed as good as any. There were many things in that book that I had never heard or been taught before about Joseph Smith and the history of the Church. This book was filled with things that I found to be contrary to the Joseph Smith I had grown to love as a child, the Joseph Smith who I believe restored the gospel of Jesus Christ. And with every turn of the page, I was met with more disappointment and discouragement. I quickly found myself down a Church history rabbit hole that I was not equipped to handle. I began questioning everything, including my own testimony and what I believed. The only way to adequately describe what I was going through is to call it a crisis of faith.

When I finished reading the book, I walked into my colleague's office, threw it down on his desk, and with tears welling up in my eyes, I blurted out, "I need to quit my job!" I sobbed as I tried to explain everything I was thinking and feeling. I was so mad. Mad about where this information had been all my life. Mad that I was lied to. Mad that I was now going to have to look for a new job because how could I possibly teach this stuff when I no longer believed in any of it? How could this have happened? Standing there in his office, I wept and at one point even fell back against a wall, slowly sliding down until falling into an almost fetal sitting position. I was so mad at my colleague for giving me that dumb book to read. Things were perfectly fine before I read that junk . . . or at least I thought so.

He silently sat at his desk and listened to me until I had no more words to speak. And then he asked me one simple question: "What did you believe before you read the book?"

I glanced at him and asked, "What do you mean?"

He said, "What did you believe was true before you read the book?"

I thought for a few minutes, then I said, "Well, I *believed* [sarcastic tone] that God lives and Jesus Christ is His Son. I believed in the Savior's Atonement and that I could be forgiven of my sins. I believed that you can get answers to your prayers, that the scriptures are the word of God, that families can be together forever . . ." Then with full emotion and tears, I said, "And I believed that Heavenly Father loves me."

He looked at me and said, "Well, what you *believed* is still true. None of that has changed. If it was true before you read the book, it's still true now. I recommended the book because there is a lot out there that you will learn, hear, and question, and that's OK. But none of that changes your truths. It's still true. It has always been true." His words in that moment brought so much clarity. He was right. What I believed before reading the book was still true, and what I wasn't sure of I needed to figure out. So, I set out to do just that. I studied more and prayed hard for a testimony of Joseph Smith. I was certain my answer would come immediately . . .

but it didn't.

The school year started, and I decided not to quit my job. With some mild reservations, I began teaching the Doctrine and Covenants and Church History. Every day that I taught, I had the lingering question, *Is Joseph Smith really a prophet of God?* About three weeks into the school year, I prepared a lesson that included reading Joseph Smith—History 1:25. After I'd taught this lesson five other times, in walked my sixth-period and last class for the day. Midway through the lesson, I asked everyone to turn to Joseph Smith—History 1:25, and rather than ask a student to read, I read it out loud to the class:

> So it was with me. I had actually seen a light, and in the midst of that light I saw two Personages, and they did in reality speak to me; and though I was hated and persecuted for saying that I had seen a vision, yet it was true; and while they were persecuting me, reviling me, and speaking all manner of evil against me falsely for so saying, I was led to say in my heart: Why persecute me for telling the truth? I have actually seen a vision; and who am I that I can withstand God, or why does the world think to make me deny what I have actually seen? For I had seen a vision; I knew it, and I knew that God knew it, and I could not deny it, neither dared I do it; at least I knew that by so doing I would offend God, and come under condemnation.

I can't fully describe what happened, but as I read those words out loud, "For I had seen a vision; I knew it, and I knew that God knew it, and I could not deny it, neither dared I do it," immediately my soul knew, and everything inside of me shouted, *IT IS TRUE!* At that moment, I knew that Joseph Smith was a prophet of God.

I looked out at my class with tears running down my face and said, "You guys . . . Joseph Smith really did see what he said he saw."

One of my students looked at me and replied, "Well duh, Sister U."

I knew it, and I knew God knew it, and I cannot deny that moment to this day. I was thirty-one years old. Ten years from the first time I stepped foot on that cliff of disbelief. At thirty-one years of age, I obtained the bread of Christ, the bread of prayer, the bread of revelation, the bread of prophecy, and the bread of the Restoration.

I learned from that experience that when we find ourselves tossed like a merchant's ship in those places that seem *afar*, we need to hang on—to continue asking, learning, questioning, testing, growing, having faith, and believing in Him. Jesus Christ calms the storms, and He is with us on our journey. Elder Jeffrey R. Holland reminded us that, no matter what the weather is on the sea of life, "a woman's abiding trust in God and unfailing devotion to things of the Spirit have always been an anchor when the wind and the waves of life were fiercest."[66] The testimony we gain during the turbulent times becomes the bread that we will feed upon when we encounter our personal famines as well as the bread that we will feed to those who are also going afar.

I did end up becoming a pretty good cook. But it wasn't the actual food I prepared daily that made a difference to my family. Instead, it was the spiritual food I obtained that they needed the most. As a result of the virtuous woman's spiritual journey, she gains a testimony of the Savior and His gospel.

Her covenants have already given her the power to do His will and nourish souls with the bread of her conversion. And the first souls she will nourish are those within her *household*.

N ☉ O T E S

15.

She riseth also while it is yet night, and giveth meat to her household, and a portion to her maidens.

15. וַתָּקָם בְּעוֹד לַיְלָה וַתִּתֵּן טֶרֶף לְבֵיתָהּ וְחֹק לְנַעֲרֹתֶיהָ:

HERE'S WHAT YOU NEED TO know about my friend Sharmaine: she's a doer. She is all about saying yes to callings and doing her best, but the one calling that stretched her beyond her limits was ward organist. She will tell you, "I'm not an organist! I can play the piano, but the organ? It's not the same thing!" That is what she told her bishop when he first asked her to be the ward organist. She was thrilled when she and her husband made the decision to move just so she could get out of that blasted calling. Well, as luck would have it, the first Sunday in her new ward, the bishop saw her at church and said, "Oh, hey, we're excited to have your family in the ward. I called your former bishop and found out you were the ward organist. We want to call you as our ward organist. How do you feel about that?" She thought, *Not great, actually*, and it took everything in her to smile and say, "Sure."

So, what does verse 15 have to do with my friend Sharmaine? The words *night, meat, household, portion,* and *maidens* may be a metaphor for something more than what it seems. We will learn how these five words played a significant role in the life of Sharmaine and how they can play a part in all of our lives.

But first, we need to know something unique about this verse. Verse 15 is distinctive in the way it is constructed. In the Hebrew text, verse 14 ends with a Hebrew ו (*vav*), which is "and," connecting verse 14 to 15 and creating a sequence of events.[67] Thus, the virtuous woman brings her food, ו (*and*) she arises at night, ו (*and*) she gives meat to her household. Biblical commentators agree that this sequence of events shows the "woman does not spare herself in supplying provisions for the household"[68] and that "the wife has imported the food; she now distributes it to her household."[69] I challenge those interpretations, and I want to take a look at these words to show what they could mean metaphorically.

She riseth also while it is yet night

Rise means to "arise, stand up, or stand up for action,"[70] and the virtuous woman does it *while it is yet night.* What makes the word *night* so incredible is that it can also be used symbolically to show "gloom or personal distress."[71] A virtuous woman knows *night.* Her voyage to obtain her food is a testament of her experience with turmoil and personal distress. Her experience and testimony qualify her to be one who will stand *while it is yet night*—and she knows what *portion* of *meat* to give.

and giveth meat to her household, and a portion to her maidens.

The word for *meat* in this verse is defined as food or something torn like the flesh of prey.[72] The symbolic meaning of *meat* in this verse can be twofold. First, it represents Christ. He is the *meat*, the spiritual nourishing power that fed the children of Israel in the wilderness (see 1 Corinthians 10:3–4).[73] Christ taught that His flesh is "meat indeed," and when we partake (through taking the sacrament, making covenants, keeping the commandments), He dwells in us and we in Him, and we become nourished (see John 6:55–57). Second, *meat* represents the Savior's work. Christ said, "My meat is to do the will of him that sent me, and to finish his work" (John 4:34). A virtuous woman fills herself with Christ's nourishing power and then, in turn, she can nourish others by doing the will of the Savior. She supports Christ's mission by doing what He would do if He were here, and she knows the exact *portion of nourishing power* to give to her *household*.

The term *household* doesn't just apply to family homes—single people have households too. Regarding the word *household*, a wise, single sister once taught:

> It seems difficult to me to create a home and make the home a learning center when living there all alone. But if you define a home by the quality of what happens there rather than the number of individuals living there, then you can exercise the faith it takes to apply the

concepts learned through lessons and mini-courses of provident living and beautifying one's surroundings, and then you can extend that faith by inviting others into your home to share in that atmosphere of warmth and learning.[74]

A virtuous woman's home is not defined by how many people live there but rather by the quality of what happens there. When you consider the meaning of *portion* and *household* and then combine those words with *maidens*, this verse might be teaching us about the quality of what happens in a virtuous woman's home and how it affects all whom she comes in contact with, regardless of age or status.

The maidens in this verse refer to young girls and suggests that the virtuous woman sees to the welfare of even the least of her household in terms of status.[75] During biblical times, women as a whole held no status or rank. Brigham Young University–Idaho professor Ross Baron taught that before marriage, a girl answered to her father. After marriage, she answered to her husband. She was obligated to obey her husband as strictly as a slave would have obeyed his or her master. There was no formal schooling for women, and they were not allowed to participate in any type of public office or to vote. Women at this time were absolutely on the margins of society to the point that the first-century Jewish man recited the following as part of his daily morning prayer: "Blessed are You, Lord our God, King of the universe, who has not created me a Gentile, a Slave or a Woman."[76] After pointing out this prayer to his audience, Professor Ross Baron then said, "That's pretty sad. Notice the order. Notice the order."[77] It seems that of the three worst things the Jewish man could have been, apparently, a woman was at the bottom of his list. When this verse says the virtuous woman gives a portion to her maidens, it is showing that, according to first-century Jewish ideology, she is no respecter of persons when it comes to who she will help. And today, as women, we too administer to and have a vested interest in any human being within our sphere of influence.

I love the word *portion* in this verse. When you give out a portion of anything, you measure out what you believe the individual needs. When an infant is learning to eat, you start with a portion size appropriate for that child. When someone is in need, a Relief Society president assesses the situation and discerns what *portion* of *meat* is appropriate. This is the primary purpose of ministering. Women today are measuring out and giving portions in so many different ways: comforting, mourning, caring, bearing one another's burdens, listening, empathizing, praying, sharing, providing a meal, babysitting, bearing testimony, and offering . . . to pay for organ lessons.

The first time Sharmaine played in her new ward, she was scared and fumbled miserably. She told me, "It was bad. Like, so bad, Tam. People are mistaken. I don't play the organ. I play the piano, and it's not the same as the organ." After the sacrament meeting was over, a sweet older woman walked up to Shar and introduced herself, "Hi. I'm Jean, the other ward organist. You did a great job today, but would you ever be interested in organ lessons? I have a friend who I take lessons from, and I could probably arrange something for you." Shar knew she needed lessons badly, so she told Jean, "Ummm, yeah. Let me check with my husband. He just started his MBA program, and I need to see if it's in our budget. It might be tricky with my kids, and I'm not sure if I have the time to take lessons. Thank you for the offer. I will let you know."

Two weeks later, Shar was in Relief Society when Jean came up to her and asked, "Have you given it any thought? Were you able to talk to your husband? See, I've been doing a lot of thinking, and I have what I call a 'slush fund' for things like this. I want to offer to pay for your lessons." Shar instantly started to cry. The woman continued, "Will that be OK for you? Can I do that for you? And I would like to babysit your children when you go to lessons. We will call it 'Pedals and Play-doh.'" Shar was speechless, and she cried some more. Through her tears, she said, "Thank you. Yes, I would like that." Shar told me, "Jean offered more than I ever expected. To pass along a teacher's name is one thing. But to offer to pay and babysit my three young children was amazing. Looking back, it was exactly what I needed during that time in my life. Being home with kids all day was sometimes isolating and hard." Shar had been battling postpartum depression, which no one knew about. Shar needed something to give her hope, and Jean was an answer to prayers. Incredibly, Jean's household included Shar, and as a result, Jean was inspired with what portion of meat to give to Shar during her night, so she gave.

A virtuous woman will stand up during anyone's night and offer a portion of whatever help she knows they need. Jean's offering to Shar was exactly what she needed. Shar took lessons for a year. At her year-end recital, she played a song *with* the foot pedals, an incredible feat for a novice, and later told me, "It was the scariest and coolest thing I have ever done!" Today, Shar is a self-proclaimed ward organist who isn't shy about letting her bishop know. President Harold B. Lee counseled, "Never is the gospel of Jesus Christ more beautiful than in times of intense need or in times of a severe storm within us as individuals, or in times of confusion and turmoil."[78] That is what we as virtuous women do for each other. Our meat is to help others during their storm because we have been there and know what portion to give. It is our nights, storms, turmoil, and tribulations that refine us and allow the Lord to use us— and use us He will.

N O T E S

NOTES

HER LABORS—VERSES 16–20

16.

She considereth a field, and buyeth it: with the fruit of her hands she planteth a vineyard.

16. זָמְמָה שָׂדֶה וַתִּקָּחֵהוּ מִפְּרִי כַפֶּיהָ נָטְעָה כָּרֶם:

I MAY HAVE LAUGHED A little too loud in the chapel when the bishop of my singles ward suggested I become a seminary teacher. I was a social worker and wasn't looking for a new job, let alone considering a complete profession transformation. I joke that I didn't really like seminary when I was in seminary; early-morning seminary had its drawbacks. But after taking the sacrament that day and pondering on the absurd suggestion, the thought *Just take the classes, what could it hurt?* entered my mind. So, I took the classes. And after six months of studying, praying, and pondering over a career change, I was interviewed by a General Authority and offered a position as a full-time seminary teacher. I had just walked into a field I had never before considered.

I wonder if the virtuous woman had a similar experience to mine in verse 16. In this verse, she considers a field, she buys it, and, she plants a vineyard on her own. What is so interesting is that the author of this proverb didn't include the husband—I can relate. You would think that he would be a part of the process of purchasing and cultivating the field, especially at a time when women were not known for owning land or having rights.[79] Looking at this verse symbolically, we can see that *considering*, *buying* and working in a *vineyard* has little to do with saving money and planting grapes and everything to do with saving souls. Teaching seminary would prove to be the same for me.

The first five verses of the proverb took a look at who the virtuous woman is. We learned about her and her household as well as her relationship with the "husband," which is the foundation for the next five verses, Quintet #2. In the following five verses, we will take a much broader look at the labors of the virtuous woman, the work she is willing to do as a result of keeping her covenants.

She considereth a field and buyeth it

The word *considereth* is זָמַם (*zamam*), which means "taking the time to consider, fix thought upon, to devise."[80] *She considereth* "implies careful pondering on the woman's part."[81] The virtuous woman has taken the time to think carefully about the vineyard; it is not a frivolous purchase. She is keenly aware of how much work it will take to maintain it. I appreciate that she is taking the time to reflect on her capacity to do good and is fixed upon a plan.

Throughout the scriptures, fields are often symbolic of the world. When the Lord explains the parable of the wheat and the tares to His disciples, He states that "the field is the world,"[82] and as Don Parry points out, the field also represents "the wicked inhabitants of the world."[83] It sounds like a pretty risky investment to me. Who would want to buy that? The word *buyeth* also means "to take or to receive."[84] In a symbolic sense, buying the field could mean taking on the responsibility of helping God's children in the wicked world, which the virtuous woman can only achieve through *the fruit of her hands*.

with the fruit of her hands she planteth

Fruit in scripture is often used to symbolize our actions, the results of our labor, and the product of our works.[85] The *fruit of her hands* refers to the work the virtuous woman will do in the field. Hands are a symbol of power, and so, when the virtuous woman *planteth*, she does so with power. Understanding the word *planteth* in this verse is essential to understanding what it is that the virtuous woman is doing. It does mean "to plant," but it also carries the figurative meaning "to establish a people."[86] Thus, the virtuous woman is helping to establish God's people and His kingdom here on earth. She is helping to establish Zion. And she is doing so with powerful hands. The blessings for doing this are amazing: "Blessed are they who shall seek to bring forth my Zion at that day, for they shall have the gift and the power of the Holy Ghost; and if they endure unto the end they shall be lifted up at the last day, and shall be saved in the everlasting kingdom of the Lamb; and whoso shall publish peace, yea, tidings of great joy, how beautiful upon the mountains shall they be" (1 Nephi 13:37). With the actions of her powerful hands, the virtuous woman will establish God's people, and she will do it in a *vineyard*.

a vineyard

The *vineyard* is a symbol for a place of spiritual labor in the house of Israel or the kingdom of God on the earth.[87] The *vineyard* is our specific place in the *field* where we were "prepared to come forth . . . to labor in his vineyard for the salvation of the souls of men" (D&C 138:56). Christ is the Lord of the vineyard and we are His servants (see Jacob 5:71–72). President Thomas S. Monson said, "Now is the time for members and missionaries to come together, to work together, to labor in the Lord's vineyard to bring souls unto Him."[88]

The Lord needs virtuous women to buy a field and to plant a vineyard with the fruit of their hands. This is our time. We are His servants. Sister Joanne B. Doxey, a former counselor in the Relief Society general presidency, reminded us: "Sisters in Zion, could there be a more rewarding calling than to labor in the Lord's vineyard for the salvation of souls?"[89] A virtuous woman thoughtfully reflects on her specific place in this world, her vineyard. She reflects on the spiritual labor she can perform there and the good she can do to establish the Lord's kingdom on this earth as she works among those who need Jesus. She is called to her specific part of the vineyard and is encouraged to do great things.

The Lord needs you to do His work in your own vineyard. But it isn't always easy to know what that means or how it will look in your life. To those who are unsure of their role in the Lord's vineyard, President Russell M. Nelson counseled:

> Ask your Heavenly Father in the name of Jesus Christ how He feels about you and

your mission here on earth. If you ask with real intent, over time the Spirit will whisper the life-changing truths to you. Record those impressions, review them often, and follow through with exactness. I promise you that when you catch even a glimpse of how your Heavenly Father sees you and what He is counting on you to do for Him, your life will never be the same! Go to the temple and listen! Listen for who you are and what you will do.[90]

Mary Musselman Whitmer found her specific place in the Lord's vineyard and was able to fix her thoughts upon what her mission was here on earth. And one of the ways she did this was by providing some string. In June 1829, Mary Musselman Whitmer and her husband, Peter, opened their home to the Prophet Joseph Smith and Oliver Cowdery so they could finish the translation of the Book of Mormon. There were already thirteen people living in the Whitmer home or on the farm. Mary was responsible for all the duties of a hostess, without any modern-day conveniences, such as a washing machine, a dryer, a dishwasher, or a pebble ice maker. Mary Whitmer was overwhelmed with all her duties, but she was blessed. Some historians refer to her as, "the Twelfth Witness" because she was shown the plates and became the only female witness to have seen them uncovered. But what I also love about her story are a few simple pieces of string.

The Book of Mormon manuscript was written on loose sheets of paper that were later sewn together with string to form bundles of pages. Decades later, the string was removed out of a necessity to conserve the pages. "The string is an important artifact that connects us not only with the manuscript itself, but also with a largely unheralded figure of the early restoration."[91] Mary Musselman Whitmer provided the string. Some believed that she may have even made it. I loved learning about the significant roles Mary played in her part of the vineyard with the fruit of her hands. Though is seems like such a small thing, her string literally held the Book of Mormon together.

I believe we are all like Mary Musselman Whitmer. I imagine each of us braiding our own proverbial piece of string, and when called upon, gladly offering it up. Each of us can contribute to the work in our specific corner of the field. We can do great things; we can make a difference, and I believe we are already doing great things. As we carefully ponder over our role, laboring for the salvation of souls in the world and in His vineyard, we will be inspired to do it in a way that is uniquely individual to us because of the way our Heavenly Father sees us and what He is counting on us to do for Him. Here's the deal: God knows that I'm not good at sharing my testimony or boldly declaring my beliefs to either a stranger on a plane or a woman to whom I have been assigned to minister. However, God does know that I respond well to a crisis. I am really good at showing support, giving someone a ride, providing a hot meal, or writing letters of recommendation. He has consistently placed people with those needs in my path. I have learned that He is perfectly aware of His children.

In Doctrine and Covenants 37, the Lord asks the Saints to move and build up another part of His vineyard—He commands them to move from New York to Ohio (D&C 37:3). This was a big commitment, and some of the Saints were hesitant. The Lord responded to those Saints through the revelation recorded in Doctrine and Covenants 38. In verses 1–8, the Lord reminds them who they are dealing with and who will help them: Him. Of all the ways He could describe Himself, I love what He says in verses 2 and 7 the most: "The same which knoweth all things, for all things are present before mine eyes . . . But behold, verily, verily, I say unto you that mine eyes are upon you. I am in your midst and ye cannot see me." The One who sees everything, whose eyes are fixed on the entire world and who is completely aware of everything . . . He sees you. He will be in your midst even if you can't see Him. Looking back, I can see how aware He was of me as a new seminary teacher. The transition was difficult. I had been assigned to take the place of a teacher that the students loved. She was the Julie Andrews of seminary teachers, "practically perfect in every way" like Mary Poppins—she could even play the guitar like Maria von Trapp. The students hated me. And while I have been known to lace stories with hyperbole, I'm not exaggerating when I say that they really did hate me.

One afternoon when school was over and I was alone in the seminary building, I lay on the floor of my classroom and sobbed. I cried out loud, asking Heavenly Father why I was led down this path. I was perfectly happy as a social worker, and people at the homeless shelter liked me . . . a lot! Heavenly Father let me have my moment, and I lay there for a while before an unexpected peace filled my soul. It was a peace that let me know I was being seen, right there on the seminary room floor. It was a peace that dried my tears. I knew in that moment that Heavenly Father was aware of me and that the decision I made to become a seminary teacher was the right one. It felt like a heavenly stamp of approval. I was exactly where I belonged in my vineyard, doing exactly what God needed me to do in the world, in exactly the way that was individual to me. After that moment, I committed to the change. I attended every single performance, play, game, meet, match, and tournament of my students. I shared my lunch, gave haircuts, wrote letters of praise to parents, and did house calls for students who were struggling. Over the course of five months, hate turned into love. I managed to create my own unique space at that school, and in the nick of time too. During the last week of school, a young woman contemplating suicide needed someone to talk to who would listen with love, and she chose me. In that moment, I was reminded God saw not just me but also my students. God is good like that. When it comes to your place in the vineyard, as you are considering, buying, and planting, He will be with you to help you accomplish His work in your specific place in His field. He will be on your right hand and on your left, His Spirit will be in your heart, and His angels will be around you (and those you serve) to bear you all up (see D&C 84:88).

NOTES

17.

She girdeth her loins with strength, and strengtheneth her arms.

17. חָגְרָה בְעוֹז מָתְנֶיהָ וַתְּאַמֵּץ זְרוֹעֹתֶיהָ:

IN THE SUMMER OF 2019, the Draper Utah Temple underwent what I would call an art beautification renovation. Several new pieces of art were added to the already existing collection on the walls of this temple, and I spent one afternoon trying to find them all. It was so cool to just stroll the floors of the temple, taking my time and looking at art. It felt like I was in the most celestial art museum ever . . . which is pretty accurate! As I walked, I found myself in a hallway that connected to some offices. I had never been there before. I rounded a corner, and on my right, I saw a large mural that I had never seen before. As I carefully examined this painting, I was overcome with emotion. The only thought that entered my mind was, "I'm just so tired," and my eyes welled with tears. The painting depicted the Savior wearily draped over a large rock beneath an olive tree in Gethsemane, looking exhausted. I imagine He had just bled from every pore, and to me, the position of His body and the fatigue on His face quietly disclosed the words, "I'm just so tired." But it wasn't over for Him.

In a few moments, Jesus would walk out of that garden, be arrested, and endure an awful night of torture and abuse without any sleep, culminating with His crucifixion, all of which would surpass any other torment known to mankind. He had to have been so tired, and yet, He would live to endure even more to accomplish the will of His Father.

What made me so emotional was that I was at a point in my life when I was "just so tired" as well. I felt like I had given my all and had nothing left to give. The moment I saw that picture, the Spirit said to me, "He gets it, and He will help you through it. You can do this." I'm not sure how long I stood there, but it was long enough for me to notice that no one walked past me for a while. I had been afforded a few moments to stand alone in the house of the Lord and be strengthened.

In verse 17, the virtuous woman "demonstrates physical strength by vast stamina. She makes herself strong, even if it was not in her nature to work so hard."[92] Based on what we have already learned about her, I think it's safe to say that the virtuous woman is strong. But I also think she's tired. Being virtuous is hard work, and sometimes it can be overwhelming. Thankfully, she doesn't have to be strong all by herself. This verse shows where a virtuous woman's strength lies and how she accesses it— it's far beyond anything she could do at a gym. We will see how the virtuous woman, with the help of her Savior, will have more than enough strength to accomplish her work in His field.

She girdeth her loins with strength

This verse begins with the word חָגַר (*chagar*), which means "to gird oneself." This alludes to an Old Testament practice done while working in the field. With a tunic or skirt on, a worker would grab hold of the back-bottom hem of the fabric and pull it up between their legs and tuck it into a belt at the front, creating loose pants. This would make working much easier. A more symbolic meaning for *gird* is "to prepare for a test of strength or other trial, muster up one's resources, set to work."[93] A virtuous woman girds herself, meaning she is ready for any test, trial, or challenge. The strength she will need comes from keeping covenants.[94]

and strengtheneth her arms

Strengtheneth in this verse refers to "physical vigor,"[95] and the word *arm* can refer to "a symbol of strength," even divine strength.[96] Because the virtuous woman is a covenant-keeping woman, her vigor comes from a divine source, the same source Nephi spoke of: "And if it so be that the children of men keep the commandments of God, he doth nourish them, *and strengthen them*, and provide means whereby they can accomplish the thing which he has commanded them" (1 Nephi 17:3; emphasis added). When we keep God's commandments, we are given the strength to do His work. This divine strength is the only thing that will help us to do all that is asked of us. This divine strength is grace.

While serving as a member of the Seventy, Elder Gene R. Cook taught, "The word *grace* is not an easy term to define. Perhaps the best definition I know is 'enabling power'; the power the Lord has given us to accomplish all things."[97]

The Apostle Paul understood God's grace and explained that it is available to all of us, even to the weakest of Saints.

When speaking of a personal trial, he called it a "thorn in the flesh" (2 Corinthians 12:7). Who can't relate to that description?! Paul asked the Lord three times for it to be removed, but it wasn't. And then the Lord said to Paul, "My grace is sufficient for thee: for my strength is made perfect in weakness" (2 Corinthians 12:8–10). The Lord's grace is sufficient, or abundant, for each of us—it's not a pie with equal-sized pieces measured out for everyone. There is enough to go around. And Christ's strength is made perfect in weakness . . . which is us, and His virtue (strength) is infinite (The Living Christ, January 1, 2000). *All* of us are the weakest of Saints, and yet how awesome is it to think that His strength or grace is made perfect in us?! When the Lord said He would extend His grace to "even the weak things of the world, those who are unlearned and despised, to thrash the nations by the power of my Spirit," He then explained what He would do with the weak things of the world: "And their arm shall be my arm, and I will be their shield and their buckler; and I will *gird up their loins*, and they shall fight manfully for me" (D&C 35:13–14; emphasis added).[98] This is strength. This is power. This is grace. Paul encouraged the Hebrews to ask for this grace when he said, "Let us therefore come boldly unto the throne of grace, that we may obtain mercy, and find grace to help in time of need" (Hebrews 4:16). As virtuous women, we can come boldly to the throne of grace and expect help through our covenants. Elder D. Todd Christofferson said, "Divine covenants make strong Christians. I urge each one to qualify for and receive all the priesthood ordinances you can and then faithfully keep the promises you have made by covenant."[99]

No matter how weak we are, what problems, difficult circumstances, or "[thorns] in the flesh" we experience in this life, it will be our covenants with and commitment to Christ that will provide us with His enabling power. One of the most incredible examples of this can be found in the stories of the pioneers. It was grace that attended every step of their journey. While experiencing their own "[thorns] in the flesh"—trials, afflictions, exhaustion, starvation, death of loved ones, and ill health or disease—it was Christ's divine strength that enabled them to take the next step.

After her conversion to the Church in Connecticut, it was the strength of nineteen-year-old Jane Manning James that led eight of her family members some 800 miles to join the Saints in Nauvoo, Illinois. In her autobiography, Jane wrote of her journey, "We walked until our shoes were worn out, and our feet became sore and cracked open and bled until you could see the whole print of our feet with blood on the ground. We stopped and united in prayer to the Lord, we asked God the Eternal Father to heal our feet and our prayers were answered and our feet were healed forthwith." On their travels, Jane and her companions were met with many trials. They faced the threat of being put in jail. They walked up to their necks in water as they crossed a river with no bridge. They spent a night in a forest out in the open air and were met the next morning with frost as thick as a light snowfall, which they walked through on bare feet. They endured all this, yet Jane still wrote, "But we went on our way rejoicing, singing hymns, and thanking God for His infinite goodness and mercy to us in blessing us as he had, protecting us from all harm, answering our prayers and healing our feet."[100]

This grace is what allowed for the Saints to make it to Utah and to settle in a place that seemed "lonely, dreary and cold."[101] Phillippa Beer Moyle's arms were strengthened, and she indeed girded her loins. Phillippa would have ten children, bury three of them, and raise the other seven practically on her own. After crossing the plains and settling in Utah, she tended to livestock and a large farm[102] on her own for most of twenty years to support her husband, John Rowe Moyle, the famed stonemason who carved the inscription "Holiness to the Lord" on the east side of the Salt Lake Temple.[103]

As we labor in the Lord's vineyard, we will be divinely strengthened, even when we are "just so tired." Paul further taught us *how* to approach the Lord and petition Him for His help: "Let us therefore come *boldly* unto the throne of grace, that we may obtain mercy, and find grace to help in time of need" (Hebrews 4:16). Because of our commitment to Christ and our covenants, His grace will strengthen our arms and help us overcome any test of strength or trial we may face. And it is through those tests and trials that our faith in and testimony of the Savior Jesus Christ can grow and benefit others.

N · O T E S

18.

She perceiveth that her merchandise is good: her candle goeth not out by night.

18. טָעֲמָה כִּי־טוֹב סַחְרָהּ לֹא־יִכְבֶּה בַלַּיְלָה נֵרָהּ׃

WHEN I BECAME A TWEEN, my parents finished our basement and gave me my own rainbow-themed bedroom. It was spectacular and sometimes inconvenient. It was across the hall from the laundry room/sewing room. I can vividly recall my mom staying up late into the night doing laundry, sewing matching dresses for all of us girls, and finishing other various projects for her family. Then, with very little sleep, she would wake up and go to work the following day.

One scholar's interpretation of verse 18 suggests that the woman is "urged on by her success so that she continues to work beyond what might normally be expected; her lamp never goes out. She seems to enjoy her labors."[104] I believe that women across the board represent this verse in its literal context. But another way to understand this verse within a scriptural context may allow for more sleep and fewer late nights spent sewing. Through this understanding, we will see that a virtuous woman's merchandise isn't something she will sell but instead represents something she offers to others. We will learn that her candle isn't a mere physical light but a spiritual light that surrounds others, motivates change, and blesses the world.[105]

She perceiveth that her merchandise is good

The virtuous woman *perceiveth*, or she טָעַם(*ta'am*), which means "to perceive or to taste."[106] In Latin, this phrase is translated as "she hath tasted and seen."[107] The virtuous woman has tasted and seen that her merchandise, what she went to such great lengths to obtain in verse 14—her testimony of Jesus Christ—is good.

Her testimony is *good*. It's not better than anyone else's or the best testimony ever. It's just good. When the earth was being formed, at the end of each day, Elohim "saw that it was *good*." But on the sixth day, after man was formed, Elohim "saw everything that he had made, and, behold, it was *very good*" (compare Genesis 1:25 to 1:31; emphasis added), which means "finished or complete."[108] Our testimonies are never finished or complete. They are works in progress and are therefore *good*. A testimony is continually developing, and we must never stop nourishing or strengthening it; this process is necessary to surviving spiritually.[109] The virtuous woman's testimony is what Elder Joseph B. Wirthlin called "a spiritual candle . . . that is needed as never before in a world enveloped in spiritual darkness."[110]

her candle goeth not out by night

Proverbs 20:27 teaches, "The spirit of man is the candle of the Lord, searching all the inner depths of his heart" (Hebrew

Translation). President Boyd K. Packer explained that the candle of the Lord is the testimony that comes during our "quest for spiritual knowledge," where there is that "'leap of faith,' as the philosophers call it. It is the moment when you have gone to the edge of the light and stepped into the darkness to discover that the way is lighted ahead for just a footstep or two."[111] On her voyage, the virtuous woman stepped into the darkness and, tapping into the innermost parts of her heart, discovered the light, *her* light, and as a result, her merchandise, her *candle*, can benefit those who are in darkness, and it *goeth not out by night*.

The phrase *her candle goeth not out by night* means "that she works well into the night."[112] But symbolically, this phrase is saying that the virtuous woman's *candle* (testimony) goeth not out by *night*. Going back to verse 15, we learned that *night* could mean "gloom or personal distress."[113] So all together, this phrase is saying her testimony will not go out during a difficult time. She is "a guide of the blind, a light of them which are in darkness" (Romans 2:19), and it is during any adversity that she will stand fast in the faith and not be moved, not only for herself but also for others because of her commitment to Christ and her covenants (1 Corinthians 16:13; D&C 87:8).

The prophet Jeremiah warned a once covenant-keeping people that if they would not hearken unto the Lord and keep their covenants, they would lose everything that mattered: "Therefore thus saith the Lord of hosts; Because ye have not heard my words . . . I will take from them the voice of mirth, and the voice of gladness, the voice of the bridegroom, and the voice of the bride, the sound of the millstones, and the light of the candle" (Jeremiah 25:8–10). Because of their wickedness, the Lord took away their joy and gladness. He removed His word and the testimony of His believers. The millstone which was used to grind wheat ceased to grind, and there was no more *food*, resulting in a physical and spiritual famine in the land. The peoples' wickedness and unwillingness to keep their covenants caused the light of their candles to go out. If we are to keep our testimonies, our candles, lit, it is vital that we keep our covenants. As we do, we will not only have light for ourselves, but we will be able to light the way for others.

Dwight Lyman Moody, a preacher from the 1800s, shared a story with his congregation about a boat in the Cleveland Harbor that was helplessly rocking and close to sinking on a stormy, starless night. The mariners on the boat could see the lighthouse, but they needed help to find their way through the narrow passage lined with treacherous rocks all around the harbor. Usually there would be lower lights or candlelit lamps on the shore that lined up with the lighthouse and marked the way to safety. But on this night, the lower lights had gone out.

The desperate captain decided he had no choice but to proceed into the harbor without the guidance of the lower lights. "With a strong hand and brave heart"—but in almost total darkness—"the old pilot turned the wheel." Tragically, he missed the channel, crashed the boat upon the rocks, and "many a life [was] lost in a watery grave."[114]

The preacher then explained the lesson to be learned from this story: the Master is the great lighthouse, but He depends on us to be the lower lights and keep them burning for any weary traveler. In attendance at that sermon was Philip Paul Bliss, the congregation's music director. He was so inspired by Moody's story that he wrote what would become one of his most famous hymns, "Brightly Beams Our Father's Mercy," (*Hymns,* no. 335).

> Brightly beams our Father's mercy
> From his lighthouse evermore,
> But to us he gives the keeping
> Of the lights along the shore.
>
> [Chorus]
> Let the lower lights be burning;
> Send a gleam across the wave.
> Some poor fainting, struggling seaman
> You may rescue, you may save.
>
> Dark the night of sin has settled;
> Loud the angry billows roar.
> Eager eyes are watching, longing,
> For the lights along the shore.
>
> Trim your feeble lamp, my brother;
> Some poor sailor, tempest-tossed,
> Trying now to make the harbor,
> In the darkness may be lost.

As lower lights, we can look to the example of the famed and gifted poet Eliza R. Snow, who was also familiar with *night*. After joining the Church, she was persecuted and cut off by family and friends. She endured the extermination order, she and her family often moving to escape the mobs, violence, and religious persecution. She cared for and sheltered her elderly parents, whom she would later bury on their journey to Winter Quarters. At the age of thirty-eight, she married Joseph Smith as a plural wife, and after two short years, Joseph was martyred in Carthage Jail. Later she became a plural wife to Brigham Young. She would never have children of her own. Through her various Church callings, including her twenty-one years as Relief Society General President, she spent her entire life serving the women of the Church.[115] Joseph F. Smith said of her, "She walked not in the borrowed light of others but faced the morning unafraid and invincible."[116]

Eliza R. Snow wrote the following beautiful lines about her light: "I will go forward . . . I will smile at the rage of the tempest, and ride fearlessly and triumphantly across the boisterous ocean of circumstance . . . And the *testimony of Jesus* will light up a lamp that will guide my vision through the portals of immortality and communicate to my understanding the glories of the Celestial kingdom."[117] A virtuous woman's candle never goes out at night because it is strong enough to triumphantly stand against any night, no matter how dark it may seem. Her candle guides others, leading them toward the only light that truly matters, the true Light that is Christ (see John 1:8).

NOTES

19.

She layeth her hands to the spindle, and her hands hold the distaff.

19. יָדֶיהָ שִׁלְּחָה בַכִּישׁוֹר וְכַפֶּיהָ תָּמְכוּ פָלֶךְ:

THIS VERSE HAS SOME UNFAMILIAR words that make it hard to understand its meaning. Spindle? Distaff? These are two instruments that are required to turn wool into yarn, which is called spinning. The female chore of spinning would typically be done during the early hours of darkness.[118] So, verse 19 is saying that the virtuous woman "weaves linen cloth from flax and wool from the fleece she has cultivated" during the night by the light of her candle that never goes out.[119] If this verse means that every woman should know how to spin wool into yarn, we have a lot of work to do. When we look at the allegorical meaning, however, we can see that this verse teaches us how to successfully keep our covenants. It shows that the symbolic spindle and distaff are an integral part of having any success; they are tools that a virtuous woman cannot do without.

She layeth her hands

The first word of this verse is יָדֶיהָ (*yada*), which means "her hand" and "indicates strength or power."[120] This word begins the phrase *She layeth her hands*, which also translates as, "She stretches out her arms to useful works."[121] To accomplish the "useful works," she will need tools, and according to this verse, she will use the *spindle* and the *distaff*.

to the spindle, and her hands hold the distaff

When it comes to the spindle and the distaff, one tool cannot be used without the other; separately, they do nothing. A virtuous woman understands that she cannot use one without the other; they go hand in hand. The spindle is a staff with a round director on the end that receives the spun wool from the distaff, which is a rod that holds the unspun wool.[122] These two tools are not mentioned anywhere else in the Bible.[123] However, we can find some spiritual parallels to them in the Book of Mormon and Doctrine and Covenants.

A "spindle" or director was given to Lehi and his family to assist them on their journey. One morning, while in the wilderness, Lehi arose and was astonished to find at his tent door "a round ball of curious workmanship" made of fine brass. Nephi explains, "Within the ball were two spindles; and the one pointed the way whither we should go into the wilderness" (1 Nephi 16:10). According to the faith of Lehi and his family, the spindle or director would tell them where to go to obtain food, and as Nephi wrote, it "did give us understanding concerning the ways of the Lord" (1 Nephi 16:29). The spindles inside the Liahona acted as a compass that showed them the way (Alma 37:38–42). Elder David A. Bednar explained the significance of a director or spindle in our own lives:

> As we each press forward along the pathway of life, we receive direction from the Holy Ghost just as Lehi was directed through the Liahona. . . . The Holy Ghost operates in our lives precisely as the Liahona did for Lehi and his family, according to our faith and diligence and heed.[124]

The director or spindle is the Holy Ghost, which has a counterpart that is fundamental to it being able to work effectively. The spindle needs the distaff. Likewise, the Holy Ghost needs revelation.

In April 1829, during the translation of the Book of Mormon, Joseph Smith received a revelation for Oliver Cowdery. In that revelation, the Lord told Oliver, "Behold thou hast a gift." He then said, "And blessed art thou because of thy gift. Remember it is sacred and cometh from above" (D&C 6:10). Oliver's gift was the gift of revelation, and by it he could "find out mysteries, that [he might] bring many to the knowledge of the truth, yea, convince them of the error of their ways" (D&C 6:11). In connection with this gift, Oliver was told of another: "Now this is not all thy gift; for you have another gift, which is the gift of Aaron" (D&C 8:6). In the original published version of this revelation, the "gift of Aaron" is instead referred to as "the gift of working with the rod."[125] Religious scholar Robert C. Fuller pointed out that during the time period in which Joseph and Oliver lived,

> there was a culture steeped in biblical ideas, language, and practices. The revelation's reference

to Moses likely resonated with him [Oliver]. The Old Testament account of Moses and his brother Aaron recounted several instances of using rods to manifest God's will (see Exodus 7:9–12; Numbers 17:8). Many Christians in Joseph Smith and Oliver Cowdery's day similarly believed in divining rods as instruments for revelation. Oliver was among those who believed in and used a divining rod.[126]

The rod of Aaron was an actual, physical rod that would allow Aaron, Moses's older brother, to perform incredible signs and wonders.[127] God explained that not only did this rod allow Aaron to receive revelation and do amazing things, but it was also a *powerful physical reminder* to Aaron to remain worthy so that he might have the gift of revelation. The same was true for Oliver Cowdery, and it can be true for us today; however, we don't need an actual rod to access the gift of revelation.

Just like the relationship between the spindle and the distaff, the Holy Ghost and revelation go hand in hand. It is impossible to successfully use one without the other. The Prophet Joseph Smith taught, "The Holy Ghost is a revelator," and "no man can receive the Holy Ghost without receiving revelations."[128] Elder David A. Bednar instructed, "Revelation is communication from God to His children on the earth and one of the great blessings associated with the gift and constant companionship of the Holy Ghost."[129] A covenant-keeping woman can access the power of the Holy

Ghost and receive revelation. As we continue to use these tools, we will become more skilled at understanding how they work, and our ability to receive revelation will increase. Elder Ronald A. Rasband taught, "If we pay attention to the promptings that come to us, we will grow in the spirit of revelation and receive more and more Spirit-driven insight and direction."[130]

Elder Rasband also taught that when ideas, thoughts, feelings, or "promptings" come to us, we need to act. This counsel begs the question, "How can I know if a thought to do something is a prompting from Heavenly Father or just some crazy idea I came up with?" The answer is this: Any thought you have that is good is from God. "And now, verily, verily, I say unto thee, put your trust in that Spirit which leadeth *to do good*—yea, to do justly, to walk humbly, to judge righteously; and this is my Spirit" (D&C 11:12; emphasis added). Do not doubt it or second-guess it; *every* good thought is from Heavenly Father, including but not limited to the thought to make chocolate chip cookies.

When I was thirty-one, I began attending a family ward after "graduating" from my singles ward for being "too old." While driving home from work one day, I had a distinct thought pop into my head: *You should make cookies for Sister Mitchell.* I started to laugh for two reasons. First, I was new in the ward, and the only thing I knew about Sister Mitchell was that she was the sweet elderly ward librarian—we weren't really friends. Second, I "knew" with absolute certainty that this idea was crazy and in no way from my Heavenly Father.

Everyone who knew me knew that I couldn't bake a decent batch of cookies if my life depended on it. Oh, I had tried on numerous occasions. I once made them for the ladies I visit taught, and my visiting teaching companion (who also happened to be my very best friend) said in the kindest words, "You know I love you, right? And you also know that I think you are an amazing person? Well, you can do a lot of incredible things, but you can't make cookies. We are not giving these to the women we visit teach." She was right. Cookies just weren't my thing. So, the thought to make cookies for Sister Mitchell was ridiculous at best. I continued driving, and the thought came again, *You need to make cookies for Sister Mitchell.* Again, I laughed and even said out loud (acknowledging that maybe it was a prompting and not some crazy random thought I was having), "Heavenly Father, you know I can't make cookies! I just can't!" I got off the freeway and headed down the road to my home, when a third time came the thought (with more insistence), "Make a plate of cookies for Sister Mitchell." I pulled into my driveway and thought, *OK, OK! You helped Noah build an ark. Surely you can help me make a decent cookie.*

I went into my kitchen, and to my utter astonishment, the cookies turned out to be delicious. My roommate came home, and after eating one she asked who brought us cookies. I told her I made them, and she just laughed and laughed, then said, "No, seriously."

I placed the cookies on a plate with a little note that said, "Dear Sister Mitchell, I was thinking about you today. Have a good day! Love, Tammy." I left them on her porch and didn't think about them or her again until Sunday at church. As I walked past the library, she quickly came toward me and grabbed my arm. She began to thank me for the cookies, and as the words came from her mouth, tears welled up in her eyes as she confided, "Those cookies made my day! It was one of the worst days of my life." I thought, *WHAT? That's saying something. Aren't you in your eighties?* Whatever that day looked like for her, I will never forget what that Sunday in front of the library looked like for me.

My limited life experience with the gift of the Holy Ghost (spindle) and revelation (distaff) guided me in the Lord's vineyard to do something as simple as making cookies. It inspired me to minister to another woman through her storm by giving her the exact portion she needed at night. The Lord even qualified my efforts by transforming my cookie-making skills! The Lord qualified me, and He will qualify all of us as we familiarize ourselves with the "spindle" and "distaff." The more we use these tools—revelation and the Holy Ghost—the more our Heavenly Parents will use us to help others.

NOTES

NOTES

20.

She stretcheth out her hand to the poor; yea she reacheth forth her hands to the needy.

‎20. כַּפָּהּ פָּרְשָׂה לֶעָנִי וְיָדֶיהָ שִׁלְחָה לָאֶבְיוֹן:

I HAVE A GOOD FRIEND who served her mission in Ukraine. One Sunday she taught a lesson in Relief Society and taught us that the words "Relief Society" in Ukrainian translate as "the Organization of Charity." Then she taught us that the word *charity* is broken down into two words: вид (*dobre*), which means "kind," and серце (*sertse*), which means "heart." In Ukrainian, the Relief Society is an "organization of kind hearts." This translation struck me. Organization of kind hearts. I belong to the Organization of Kind Hearts. On March 17, 1842, twenty kind hearts gathered in the upper room of Joseph Smith's Red Brick Store in Nauvoo, Illinois, with Joseph Smith, John Taylor, and Willard Richards. Their names were Mrs. Emma Smith, Mrs. Sarah M. Cleveland, Phoebe Ann Hawkes, Elizabeth Jones, Sophia Packard, Philinda Merrick, Marth Knights, Desmonda Fulmer, Elizabeth Ann Whitney, Leonora Taylor, Bathsheba W. Smith, Phebe M. Wheeler, Elvira A, Co[w]les, Margaret A. [Norris] Cook, Athalia Robinson, Sarah M. Kimball, Eliza R. Snow, Sophia Robinson, Nancy

Rigdon, and Sophia Marks.[131] This meeting established an organization of women called the Nauvoo Female Benevolent Society. Because President Emma Smith did not like the name that had been decided on, she "suggested that she would like an argument with Elder Taylor on the words Relief and Benevolence."[132] After a debate over the two words and pointing out the negative connotation that *benevolent* had at that time (Washingtonian Benevolent Society, a corrupt institution of that day), it was decided and agreed that the name would be the Female Relief Society of Nauvoo. In support of the word *relief*, President Emma Smith said, "We are going to do something extraordinary—we expect extraordinary occasions and pressing calls."[133] For over 175 years, this kindhearted organization has participated in extraordinary occasions and has answered pressing calls. To every woman belonging to the Organization of Kind Hearts, verse 20 is understood with clarity. The Relief Society organization was set up to stretch out hands offering relief to the poor and needy. During that March 17th meeting Joseph Smith said that the Relief Society is "not only to relieve the poor, but to save souls"[134] and the Hebrew definition of *poor* and *needy* invites us to do exactly that.

She stretcheth out her hand to the poor; yea she reacheth forth her hands to the needy

Poor can mean someone who is "afflicted, depressed in mind or circumstance."[135] *Needy* not only refers to those in want, but also those "subject to oppression and abuse."[136] These *poor* and *needy* are the poorest and neediest of us all. Elder Jeffrey R. Holland defined them as "those who are facing personal trials and family struggles, those who endure conflicts fought in the lonely foxholes of the heart, those trying to hold back floodwaters of despair that sometimes wash over us like a tsunami of the soul."[137]

When we stretch our hands out to the poor and needy, we go beyond meeting their physical needs. We are saving souls by bringing them to Christ. So, what does this look like in real life? Bringing souls to Christ begins with an invitation, and this invitation to come unto Christ is the most important invitation we could ever offer another person. Elder Henry B. Eyring said this about the invitation:

> It is the most important invitation anyone could accept. From the beginning of the Restoration of the gospel in this dispensation, it has been the charge given by Jesus Christ to His representatives. . . . Every member of the Church, upon accepting the baptismal covenant, becomes a disciple who has promised to stand as a witness of Jesus Christ at all times in any place he or she may be in. The purpose of our witness is to invite people to come unto Him.[138]

Please don't worry if this seems overwhelming or if you're uncertain about where to begin or what to do. Inviting others to come unto Christ is not meant to be difficult or uncomfortable. It can even be done without a lot of fanfare.

In the Old Testament, there is an incredible story about a man named Naaman, the commander of the king's army and an honorable, great, and mighty man of valor—but he had recently become a leper. Being a leper meant that he was unclean, and according to the law of Moses, he would be sent to live a life in isolation and embarrassment. Naaman had successfully delivered Syria from the enemy and was afforded the spoils of war. One of his spoils was a little Israelite girl who became his wife's maid. This little maid heard about Naaman's leprosy and knew what would help him. She spoke twenty words to her mistress that changed everything: "Would God my lord were with the prophet that is in Samaria! for he would recover him of his leprosy" (2 Kings 5:1–3). Those twenty words spoken by this little maid eventually led Naaman to seek out the prophet Elisha and to be healed of his leprosy. This miracle then caused Naaman to exclaim, "Now I know that there is no God in all the world except in Israel" (2 Kings 5:15 NIV). The little maid's simple testimony was an invitation to the poor and needy Naaman to come unto Christ, and it worked.

Moroni's very last words in the Book of Mormon were an invitation for everyone to "come unto Christ, and be perfected in him" (Moroni 10:32). Moroni's short invitation teaches us that by coming to Christ, we can be healed and perfected. The invitation from Jesus to "come unto me" is estimated by Elder James E. Talmage to be one of the "grandest outpourings of spiritual emotion known to man."[139] The Savior said, "Come unto me, all ye that labour and are heavy laden, and I will give you rest. Take my yoke upon you, and learn of me; for I am meek and lowly in heart: and ye shall find rest unto your souls. For my yoke is easy and my burden is light" (Matthew 11:28–30).

We are invited to take His yoke upon us, which happens to be easy and light—easier and lighter than what we are currently carrying. This popular quote is often considered to be a message from Christ: "I never said it would be easy, I only said it would be worth it."[140] But it's wrong! Christ *did* say it would be easy! It will be easy because His yoke is easy and He will carry it with us.

A yoke is a wooden crosspiece fastened to the backs of two animals so they can pull a load together. A yoke balances the burden, making it easier to pull, but it does not remove the load. We as mortals, or the natural man, often try to carry our yokes alone. But the burdensome load of the yokes we each carry will become lighter with the Savior because He will carry it with us. He is by our side as we brace for the tsunami of despair. Elder David A. Bednar explained how this is done: "Making and keeping sacred covenants yokes us to and with the Lord Jesus Christ. In essence, the Savior is beckoning us to rely upon and pull together with Him, even though our best efforts are not equal to and cannot be compared with His. As we trust in and pull our load with Him during the journey of mortality, truly His yoke is easy and His burden is light. We are not and never need be alone."[141]

Because the Savior is the only one who knows "according to the flesh how to succor his people according to their infirmities" (Alma 7:12), He is the only one who can effectively pull with us. *Succor* literally means to run to give aid or help. This is not a figure of speech. The Savior will come running to us. He even came running to me in my closet.

After getting married at the ripe age of thirty-four years, eight months, and twenty-two days, it didn't take long for me to realize how difficult being a stepmom was. I was a bride for our five-day honeymoon, and then I woke up a mom. After about nine months, things started to "get real," and I found myself failing miserably at this new mom thing. After a very difficult and emotional day trying to "mother" two little girls who were grieving the loss of their mother, adjusting to their dad getting remarried, and trying to figure out the new mom thing too, I hid in my closet, fell to my knees, and wept. I was deeply depressed to say the least. I was certain I had made a mistake by even getting married and that I just wasn't cut out for marriage and motherhood. That day in my closet, I pleaded, sobbed, negotiated for a different situation, petitioned for change, cried some more, looked around for the easiest items to pack, and wondered how fast I could leave my new family . . . and then my husband walked in.

I quickly stood up, feeling totally embarrassed. He could clearly tell that something was wrong.

"The girls told me you were in here. What's up?"

"I just don't think I can do this anymore. I'm not a good enough mom; I don't have what it takes. I'm failing at this whole mom thing. I think I made a mistake, and I don't know what to do about it." My husband lovingly listened and didn't try to fix it or offer suggestions. After my deluge of words and tears had finally come to an end, he looked at me, put out his hand to shake mine, and said, "Well, I want to thank you for giving it a shot." I stared in disbelief at his response and then burst out laughing. He hugged me and offered consoling words, assuring me that I was doing a really great job, given the circumstances. We talked, and I *graciously* agreed to stay and give it another shot. This may sound odd, but those eleven words spoken by my husband were the invitation I needed to laugh, give myself a break, and get on my knees later that night and humbly ask Jesus for help.

I was a bit skeptical and pretty certain that Jesus didn't know how to help me. After all, He's never been a stepmom. It turns out I was wrong. Out of nowhere, an idea would pop into my head that would help whichever daughter needed it. I felt calm when I wanted to yell. I walked away when I wanted to engage. I felt love when I was justified to hate. Jesus carried the yoke with me and, as it turns out, Jesus's yoke *is* easier and lighter than what I had been so used to carrying. He lifted that heavy and uncomfortable yoke off my neck, the yoke that I had solely, tearfully, and wearily carried into my new life, and then He affectionately put His yoke in its place. And because Jesus did that for me, I was now in a position to help others. Elder Neal A. Maxwell explained, "Jesus is the exemplar. While shouldering Jesus's yoke, we, too, can better come to 'know according to the flesh how to succor [each other].'"[142]

I found it easier to empathize with other moms who were struggling. I inherently knew what portion of bread to give someone who needed it because I had been poor and needy myself. The Lord had come running to me in the lonely closet of my heart. Clothing, shoes, dirty laundry, and all, He was there offering me the exact portion that I needed. At that moment,

I felt like the poorest and neediest of God's daughters, but turning to Him made all the difference. A virtuous woman is able to succor others. She is running to give aid to those in lonely places. She is helping the poor and needy find their way to Christ and is teaching them, in her own way, how to accept His invitation to come unto Him. She reacheth out her hands to the poor and needy, offering the help that the Savior would give if He were here by shouldering the yoke of those who are afflicted, depressed in mind or circumstance, or subject to oppression and abuse. A virtuous woman's kind heart is enough, and it is exactly what the Lord needs to help others to come unto Him.

NOTES

HER COVERINGS—
VERSES 21–25

21.

She is not afraid of the snow for her household: for all her household are clothed with scarlet.

21.לֹא־תִירָא לְבֵיתָהּ מִשָּׁלֶג כִּי כָל־בֵּיתָהּ לָבֻשׁ שָׁנִים:

I WAS A BIT OF a late bloomer when it came to dating and boys. The only high school dance I ever got asked to was homecoming my senior year, and you'd better believe my parents pulled out all the stops to make it as big of a deal as I thought it was. They even offered to buy me a new dress. We spent countless hours trying to find the perfect dress, but nothing fit right or was modest enough for my tastes. So, we decided to make my dress. OK, well, my mom offered to make it for me since I had zero sewing skills. We found a pattern that resembled a Jessica McClintock dress (a very trendy style at the time), and we drove to a fancy fabric store in downtown St. Louis, Missouri. I knew my fabric the moment I saw it: scarlet-colored crushed velvet. It was divine. My mom sewed for many days and well into many nights to make this dream come true. The pièce de résistance was the long, white, lace bib piece that flowed from my neck to my belly button. I looked smashing. At that point in my life, it was the most beautiful I had ever felt, and according to verse 21, I was also like the virtuous woman . . . well, sort of.

The following quintet focuses on what a virtuous woman is wearing or covered in. But it isn't about a scarlet-colored Jessica McClintock knockoff dress or fancy clothes. These next five verses teach us that our coverings are symbols of the covenants we make with the Husband. They not only commit us to being unshakable in our devotion to God but also serve as a reminder to us that God will always be unshakable in His devotion toward us.[143]

She is not afraid of the snow for her household

In this verse, *snow* has dual symbolism. First, it is symbolic of the cold and represents a physical death.[144] The Bible often uses deep and falling snow to describe hardships or death.[145] Next, the color of snow is "a statement of triumph of the spirit over the flesh, of good over evil, of overcoming the spiritual death that is caused by sin."[146] David used this simile when he pled for forgiveness: "Purge me with hyssop, and I shall be clean: wash me, and I shall be whiter than snow" (Psalm 51:7). This dual symbolism teaches us that snow can represent both physical death and spiritual death. While physical death is difficult to comprehend, painful to watch, and often leaves us without answers, it seems that spiritual death weighs even more profoundly on our hearts. With physical death, there is an absolute guarantee of a resurrection for everyone; we will live again, see our loved ones again. However, the finality of spiritual death is devastating. But a virtuous woman is not afraid of this "snow" because *all of her household are clothed with scarlet.*

for all her household are clothed with scarlet

Scarlet was an expensive cloth mainly afforded to the wealthy.[147] However, in scripture, the shades of scarlet, red, and crimson are most often used as symbols of the Atonement of Jesus Christ, which is available to everyone. The color symbolizes Christ's blood that was shed. Sometimes the color is linked to life, death, resurrection, and evil, all of which have close ties to the Savior and our need for His atoning sacrifice.[148] A virtuous woman's household is covered in the knowledge of this truth and the blessings that come from it. A clear and wonderful example of this is found in the Book of Mormon.

The two thousand stripling warriors were young men of the Anti-Nephi-Lehies who decided to go to war. They had no experience or knowledge of how to fight: "Now they never had fought, yet they did not fear death; and they did think more upon the liberty of their fathers than they did upon their lives" (Alma 56:47). Roughly thirteen years earlier, the people of Anti-Nephi-Lehi, after becoming converted and burying their weapons of war, were attacked by the Lamanites, and 1,005 of them were killed (Alma 24:16–22). The mothers of these two thousand stripling warriors had most likely come to know physical death on a very personal level. They had experienced the grief that accompanies the loss of a loved one, yet they were not afraid to send their sons into battle. The boys' testimonies were the only weapons that would conquer all. Their mothers had armed them with the knowledge of Jesus Christ's Atonement. Those young men "were exceedingly valiant for courage and also for strength and activity; but behold, this was not all—they were men who were true at all times in whatsoever thing they were entrusted . . . They had been taught to keep the commandments of God and to walk uprightly before him" (Alma 53:20–21).

Those boys believed that their God was with them and that "he will not suffer that we should fall; then let us go forth" (Alma 56:46). As those young men headed into battle, they were clothed in scarlet because their mothers taught them "that if they did not doubt, God would deliver them" (Alma 56:47). They did not fear death even when death was staring them in the face because, as they boldly declared, "We do not doubt our mothers knew it" (Alma 56:48). Indeed, these mothers and sons were praying and hoping for a physical deliverance, but even if they could not be delivered, they knew they could escape spiritual death through Christ, the Redeemer of the world. They trusted in the Husband, who possesses the power to conquer death and redeem all mankind from the Fall and from the grasp of Satan.[149] The Atonement of Jesus Christ offers hope and a surety that these words declared by Elder Neal A. Maxwell will one day be fulfilled: "Righteous sorrow and suffering carve cavities in the soul that will become later reservoirs of joy."[150] I witnessed a very real example of this with my friend Tami.

A few years ago, my friend Tami and her husband, Mike, surprised their three oldest children with a Christmas trip to Disneyland. They decided to leave their two toddlers behind with their grandma during the short five-day trip. While away, their two-year-old daughter Joy became sick and died in the night while in the care of her sweet grandmother. A rare virus had attacked her lungs and went undetected while they had been treating her croupy cough. Imagine my friend's sorrow and anguish as she received that phone call from nine hundred miles away. They packed up the car, raced to Idaho, and after a few days there, they had their little girl's body transported back to Utah. When they arrived home without their daughter Joy, their oldest daughter, who was ten, suggested that they take time as a family to read the scriptures and pray. Mike randomly opened the scriptures to John 16, which happened to be the chapter where the Savior tells of His imminent death and resurrection. Verses 20–22 leaped off the page and into their aching hearts:

> Verily, verily, I say unto you, that ye shall weep and lament, but the world shall rejoice: and ye shall be sorrowful, but your sorrow shall be turned into joy.
>
> A woman when she is in travail hath sorrow, because her hour is come: but as soon as she is delivered of the child, she remembereth no more the anguish, for joy that a man is born into the world.
>
> And ye now therefore have sorrow: but I will see you again, and your heart shall rejoice, and your joy no man taketh from you.

The night before the funeral, Tami made a surprising request: she asked me and another close friend to go with her to the funeral home to be alone with her baby Joy one last time before the crowds came and the day of mourning began. Together, and mostly in silence, we drove to the funeral home. It was late, and very few people were there. We were escorted to the room where Joy was. With great apprehension, I opened the door, and we walked into the dimly lit room. On the far side of the room was a tiny casket where baby Joy's lifeless body lay. She was dressed in angelic white with a bow in her hair and her thumb still in the sucking position where it had been when they found her.

My dear friend walked over to the casket, lifted her sweet baby out of it, and brought her over to where we were standing. We sat down with Tami between us, and we held this lifeless little baby across our laps. My friend's sorrow had been silent up until that moment, when she began to shed a tsunami of tears. They were hers to shed. It would have been well within her right to fall on the ground as she cradled that little body and, in anguish, curse God, yelling at the inhumanity and unfairness of it all while shaking her fists in the air, questioning God's hand in her life and in the life of her baby. But she didn't. Instead, she slowly and lovingly caressed Joy's cheeks. She kissed her face. She lifted that little body and took in the deepest breath, saying, "I don't want to forget her smell." She held those tiny hands one last time, touching every little finger as she shed the tears of a grieving mother. That night, with very few words, she mourned the loss of her little girl.

In that sacred moment at the funeral home, the two of us who were privileged to be a part of such a hallowed experience were clothed in scarlet. Tami clothed us in her testimony of Jesus Christ's power to overcome death, of the Father's unfailing plan of happiness—even when it wasn't so happy. To this day, as a virtuous woman, she continues to cover us and those who are among her household in scarlet—her witness of the Savior's Atonement.

Since that day at the funeral home, I have watched my friend and her family mourn the loss of little Joy as well as rejoice in the glory that they will one day be reunited with her. As excruciating as this has been for her, she feels no sense of fear associated with Joy's death, only hope in an eternal life. It hasn't been easy, but her testimony of the Resurrection has buoyed her family up during moments that would otherwise have drowned them. My virtuous friend who buried her daughter is confident in the Savior's promises. I have watched her plead for and receive the peace the Savior offers all of us.

Tami's family has deep and abiding love for the Savior and sure testimonies of His unfailing plan. Because of Tami's faith, her household has hope in Christ's grace, and they await the day when they will rejoice in the goodness of the Father and in the Son's glory. Tami has been promised "Joy" for all her household.[151]

NOTES

22.

She maketh herself coverings of tapestry; her clothing is silk and purple.

22. מַרְבַדִּים עָשְׂתָה־לָּהּ שֵׁשׁ וְאַרְגָּמָן לְבוּשָׁהּ׃

HAVE YOU EVER SEWN ANYTHING before? Did you take a sewing class in high school where you were required to make a pillowcase or pajama pants? The first thing I learned to sew was an apron. The second thing: pockets. Once I discovered how easy it was to sew on pockets, nine-year-old me jumped on that new skill, proudly presenting my mom with a Mother's Day gift fit for anyone with twelve hands or twelve things needing a safe place . . . all in the same apron. I didn't exactly excel at sewing, and thankfully, this verse has nothing to do with selecting fabric, threading a needle, or dressing incredibly well. In verse 21, the virtuous woman covers herself and her household in scarlet, but here in verse 22, what else is being covered and made?

She maketh herself coverings of tapestry

The *coverings* a virtuous woman makes in this verse are a tapestry, coverlet, or bedspread.[152] This word could simply be teaching us that she made a bedspread and put it on her bed. Still, I really like what a seventeenth-century theologian believed about the phrase: "It may signify the ordinances of the Gospel, and the decent, orderly, and beautiful administration of them, wherein the church has communion with her Lord."[153] The tapestry in this verse could be a symbol of discipleship.

Elder Robert D. Hales pointed out that "weaving the spiritual tapestry of personal discipleship requires more than a single thread."[154] Every day we live, we are weaving the threads of this tapestry. Each thread in the virtuous woman's tapestry is a culmination of the work she has done in verses 11–20. Wonderfully woven together are her threads of service, righteousness, obedience, consecration, sacrifice, humility, and charity, along with the deeds she has done and the commandments and covenants she has kept. She has truly become a disciple. And everything the tapestry represents is also evident in the clothing that she wears.

her clothing is silk and purple

Silk in this verse is defined as fine linen, something that is bleached and dyed white, used in the tabernacle, and symbolizes purity and righteousness.[155] The Apostle John saw the coming of the Lord, calling it "the marriage supper of the Lamb" (Revelation 19:9) and wrote that those in attendance will be wearing "fine linen, clean and white: for the fine linen is the righteousness of saints" (Revelation 19:8).

Besides the white linen, the virtuous woman is said to be wearing purple, which represents wealth, power, and royalty.[156] Proverbs 12:4 teaches that "a virtuous woman is a crown to her husband." We, as virtuous women, are Christ's crown, thus, the symbol of His royalty. This color also symbolizes the virtuous woman's divinity as a spiritually begotten daughter of Heavenly Parents. A virtuous woman's righteousness, purity, divinity, and royalty are all woven throughout her tapestry of discipleship. These two colors play an important role in her overall story leading up to being covered or wrapped by the Savior in a tapestry that is unique to Him.

When I returned home from my mission, I walked off the plane fully expecting a crowd of loved ones, friends, ward members, neighbors, the mailman, and my high school band, all anxiously awaiting my return. I was certain there would be a massive crowd with balloons and signs cheering my name for a job well done. Everyone would be hollering, "You did it! We are so proud of you!" Instead, the only person I saw was my bishop. He welcomed me home with a hug, and after looking around for my family, we both hunched our shoulders and headed for the baggage claim. As we walked, I could hear music being played in the distance behind me. I noticed it, but not enough to turn around. As we continued to walk, the music grew louder and louder. *Oh,* I thought, *I know that song. That's Neil Diamond singing my favorite song. That's the song my sisters and I have a dance routine to. That's . . .* And then I heard a squeal of delight and a "Welcome home, Tam!" I turned around, and there was my family with balloons, a huge sign, and a ghetto blaster on my dad's shoulder playing my song.

I saw my parents and immediately burst into tears, falling into their arms in an embrace I will never forget. Everything about that embrace shouted, "Job well done! You did it! We are so proud of you!" That hug was a culmination of the tapestry I had woven for the last eighteen months, the last five-hundred-forty-seven days and two Christmases. Everything I thought I had lost or missed out on was made up for in that moment. I had no regrets for going. I believe this is how it will be when we see Christ and our Heavenly Parents again. Similar to my mission homecoming, an Old Testament practice also shares some similarities with this joyful future reunion.

During Old Testament times, if someone was fleeing for their life in the desert and needed protection, it was custom for them to seek shelter in the tent of a great sheikh. Pleading for their life, the fleeing individual would walk up to the tent door and say, "*Ana dakhiluka*," which means "I am thy suppliant,"[157] (beggar or petitioner). The sheikh, kinsman, or lord of the tent could then choose to offer protection or send the desperate, pleading traveler on his way. If the lord chose to offer help, he would take the hem of his robe and wrap it around the person's shoulder or over his whole body and declare that he would have protection.[158] The beggar would then enter into a covenant with the lord, promising his loyalty and fidelity to his new kinsman. In return, the lord or kinsman promised the man kinship privileges: safety, protection, and redemption from debts and/or slavery.

This is not just an ancient custom; this is our story too. Jesus Christ is our divine kinsman, and the practice of begging the Lord for His help and being covered by Him is familiar to all who have experienced the miracle of Christ's Atonement.[159] As disciples of Christ, we cry out to our Lord

"Ana dakhiluka," or "I am thy suppliant," or "I am prayerfully petitioning thee, Lord." He invites us into His tent, His house, His temple, and *covers* us with His robe.[160] And what's even more beautiful is that He not only covers us but embraces us.

Nephi begged for this covering or embrace when he prayed, "O Lord, wilt thou *encircle me around* in the robe of thy righteousness! O Lord, wilt thou make a way for mine escape before mine enemies!" (2 Nephi 4:33; emphasis added). Shortly before Lehi's passing, he told his family, "The Lord hath redeemed my soul from hell, I have beheld his glory, and I am encircled about eternally in the arms of his love" (2 Nephi 1:15). Mormon spoke of this close embrace when he wrote that the wicked "might have been clasped in the arms of Jesus" (Mormon 5:11) if they would repent.

The Lord does not hold His arms out straight, offering a hand to shake. Instead, His arms are curved outward, prepared to give a hug. The virtuous woman is encircled eternally in the arms of His love. Her tapestry and the colors white and purple represent the life she has lived and her kinship to the Divine Kinsman. Like the virtuous woman, we come to Him begging and pleading for His safety, mercy, love, and redemption. He will not turn us away. He will place His protecting tapestry around our shoulders, and He will embrace us. Our spiritual tapestry and worshipful clothing of silk and purple are proof of our belief, discipleship, redemption, and love for the Lord. At that moment, nothing will be lost. It will have all been worth it. That embrace will be a culmination of the tapestry we have woven, a resounding shout of, "Job well done! You did it! We are so proud of you!"

NOTES

23.

Her husband is known in the gates, when he sitteth among the elders of the land.

23. נוֹדָע בַּשְּׁעָרִים בַּעְלָהּ בְּשִׁבְתּוֹ עִם־זִקְנֵי־אָרֶץ:

TEN-YEAR-OLD TAMMY HAD HER LIFE all planned out. Grow up, graduate from high school, and marry Ricky Schroeder. End of plan. It was so simple and so perfect, and it would have fit in nicely with the content of verse 23. Ricky was well-known, and after growing old together, he would still be well-known . . . while sitting . . . and I guess talking to the other elders in the land? What does verse 23 even mean?

Here the husband is mentioned for the first time in the proverb since verse 11. There are some conflicting interpretations of this verse. Some scholars consider the husband's role inconsequential, with the male reduced to the edges of the property, while others see the husband as playing a significant community role.[161] But looking at it symbolically, verse 23 could be echoing lyrics from a hymn: "There was no other good enough to pay the price of sin. He only could unlock the gate of heav'n and let us in."[162]

Her husband is known in the gates

The Husband, or Jesus Christ, is *known*, which is the first word of this verse, נודע (*nowda*).[163] The phrase "to be known in" refers to "being respected, recognized and praised."[164] As one eighteenth-century theologian put it, Christ was known in "the dignity of his person, in the excellency of his offices, and the fulness of his grace; He is known by them in the relation of an husband; He is well known in the Church of God, in the assembly of his saints, *He is known in the gates of Zion.*"[165]

During biblical times, gates were a symbol of protection and were known as the threshold or entrance into a city. They were also a place of teaching, debate, and judgment: "Judges and officers shalt thou make thee in all thy gates, which the Lord thy God giveth thee, throughout thy tribes: and they shall judge the people with just judgment" (Deuteronomy 16:18; 17:8–13). As a place of judgment, it was "where courts of justice were kept, and causes heard and tried by the judges, the elders of the land."[166] It was believed that "anciently, kings sat in judgment at the gates, probably as sacred places of divine power."[167]

The Book of Mormon prophet Jacob taught, "The keeper of the gate is the Holy One of Israel; and he employeth no servant there; and there is none other way save it be by the gate" (2 Nephi 9:41) because there is no one else who can take His place. No one else who can do the job. No one else who knows not just our works, but the desire of our hearts (D&C 137:9). Jesus Christ is at the gate and awaits our return to offer us protection, to stand as our advocate before the judgment bar of God. With the elders of the land, He sits upon a throne at the gate to welcome in future heirs to their thrones.

when he sitteth among the elders of the land

Historically, the term *elder* referred to "men of mature years and experience, who were appointed to act as magistrates in the towns and as judges in the ecclesiastical tribunals."[168] Rather than an office in the Melchizedek Priesthood, in the Old Testament, this term is used to describe "a level of organization in Israel and in some circumstances, these elders appeared as religious leaders; at other times, they functioned in civil matters."[169] The *elders* in this proverb verse are the "elders of the earth." They are Abraham, Isaac, and Jacob. It is these elders who sit with the *Husband* because they have made promises and covenants with Him. These great patriarchs have become exactly like God, for "they have entered into their exaltation, according to the promises, and sit upon thrones, and are not angels but are gods" (D&C 132:37).[170] At the gates, these *elders of the land* "sit upon thrones" with the Savior, awaiting our arrival. These men of mature years, with experience over religious and civil matters, await our arrival when we will be invited to sit with them. Our RSVP to this invitation is solely through our use of Jesus Christ's Atonement.

A common way to explain the word *atonement* is to break it down into its three separate syllables—"at-one-ment"— meaning to become "at one" with God. However, I love the

Hebrew word for *atonement, kaphar*, which means "to cover, make propitiation, atone for sin."[171] Think of all the situations in your life that involve being covered. When the "covers" on a bed offer warmth and comfort. When you can't pay a bill or are in another tough situation and ask a friend, "Hey, can you cover me?" When that friend assures you, "I'll cover you." The Savior's Atonement offers these same things. It covers us when our debt to justice far outweighs the price of mercy and we come up short. It offers warmth and comfort in all of life's unpleasantly frigid and often lonesome situations. The Savior certainly has our backs in the face of any danger, even the very jaws of hell (see D&C 122:7). Christ's Atonement will always *cover* us, and Yom Kippur is an annual holy day set apart by the Jews to celebrate and honor this gift.

Yom Kippur means "Day of Atonement" and is the holiest day of the year. It is a Sabbath day, and Jews worldwide spend the day in fasting and prayer, seeking forgiveness for sins committed during the past year. It is customary to wear white on this holiday, symbolizing purity and that one's "sins shall be as white as snow" (Isaiah 1:18). There are two Hebrew words that can teach us the significance of both this holiday and the Atonement itself: תשובה (*Teshuva*) and ישבה (*Yeshuva*). These words teach us the blessings that come from repentance. Hugh Nibley taught, "*Teshuvah* is to return back to God, to return home; it's when you return and are let in. *Yeshuvah* is when you sit down or *Yashab*, which means to sit down beside your Lord. In one you return home, and in the other you enter the tent and sit down beside your Lord."[172] The Book of Mormon teaches us about this:

- Behold, my brethren, do ye suppose that such an one can *have a place to sit down in the kingdom of God, with Abraham, with Isaac, and with Jacob*, and also all the holy prophets, whose garments are cleansed and are spotless, pure and white? I say unto you, Nay; except ye make our Creator a liar from the beginning, or suppose that he is a liar from the beginning, ye cannot suppose that such *can have place in the kingdom of heaven*; but they shall be cast out for they are the children of the kingdom of the devil. (Alma 5:24–25; emphasis added)

- And may the Lord bless you, and keep your garments spotless, that ye may at last be brought *to sit down with Abraham, Isaac, and Jacob*, and the holy prophets who have been ever since the world began, having your garments spotless even as their garments are spotless, in the kingdom of heaven to go no more out. (Alma 7:25; emphasis added)

- And land their souls, yea, their immortal souls, *at the right hand of God in the kingdom of heaven, to sit down with Abraham, and Isaac, and with Jacob*, and with all our holy fathers, to go no more out. (Helaman 3:30; emphasis added)

- That when he shall finish his work I may receive him unto myself, even as I did my servant David Patten, who is with me at this time, and also my servant Edward Partridge, and also my aged servant Joseph Smith, Sen., who sitteth with Abraham at his right hand, and blessed and holy is he, for he is mine. (D&C 124:19)

The only way any of us will qualify for Teshuva and Yeshuva is if we repent and allow for the Savior's kaphar to cover us. We will need to do this many times throughout our lives, and there may be times when being covered will be uncomfortable.

I was twenty-one years old the first time I repented. Sure, I had repented before, but this was a BIG repentance—the kind that required the assistance of a priesthood leader. I grew up convinced of the idea that if I ever told my bishop anything, every Sunday, he would look at me from the podium and think, "I know what you did, you little jerk. And I'm going to tell your mom. And you'll probably get grounded." So, there was no way I was ever going to talk to anyone about anything that I had ever done. When I had arrived at my mission in Fresno, California, my mission president, President Bott, hosted a dinner and an incoming missionary fireside that night. The only thing I remember from his talk was him saying that if any of us needed to take care of past sins that hadn't been taken care of before coming, all we needed to do was call him and say, "I need to kick a can around the block." I remember it because immediately I looked around the room and thought, *Wow. I wonder who that was for.*

After two weeks of being a missionary I was ready to give up the fight. They were the two worst weeks of my life, and I knew I needed to "kick a can around the block." Fourteen days straight, my mind was plagued with thoughts like, *You're not*

*worthy to be here. You're disgusting. God doesn't love you. You're
a hypocrite. Teaching people about repentance and Jesus Christ.
Pfffffftt, what do you know about that?* I was so overwhelmed and
burdened with shame from every single thing I had ever done
in my twenty-one years of life that I was spiritually paralyzed,
and in good conscience, I could no longer serve a mission. I
made the call, and President Bott was at my apartment within
twenty minutes. He knocked, I opened the door, and without
hesitation or a greeting, he said, "Let's go kick that can."

We walked out onto the driveway, and he said to me,
"OK. Here's what I want you to do: take your bucket of yuck
and pour it all out. Tell me everything."

With that, my eyes immediately filled with tears, and I
began to weep. I told him, "I can't. I just can't. Every time
you see me, you are going to know everything I did, and you
are going to hate me."

President Bott rolled his eyes and said, "You dummy.
Don't you know how the repentance process works?" I didn't.
He then told me to go back into my apartment and get my
scriptures. After I retrieved them, he said, "Turn to Doctrine
and Covenants 58:42–43 and read it out loud."

I read those verses: "Behold, he who has repented of his
sins, the same is forgiven, and I, the Lord, remember them no
more. By this ye may know if a man repenteth of his sins—
behold, he will confess them and forsake them." I assured him
that I had "forsaken." I had been a stupid kid. I hadn't really
known or understood, but I had forsaken my sins, and now I
was ready to confess.

He rolled his eyes again and said, "You missed the most important verse. Read verse 42 again.

"Behold, he who has repented of his sins, the same is forgiven, and I, the Lord, remember them no more."

Well, no duh. I at least knew that much about repentance. I knew that God didn't remember my sins anymore.

Then my mission president taught me the most profound lesson of my life: "Sister Uzelac, if God doesn't remember your sins anymore, why would He give a puny man like me here on earth more power than He has? If God doesn't remember them anymore, neither do I."

WHAT?!

Since that day on my mission, I have asked every mission president, stake president, and bishop I've met if that is true. Unequivocally, they all agree that it is.

I looked at President Bott and said, "Let's go kick that can!"

We walked around the block, and when we got back to the driveway, he asked, "Is that everything?"

I said, "No, it's not," and so we walked around again. He spent an hour with me that day listening, explaining, and listening some more. He told me that many of the things I confessed weren't sins at all because I was acted upon by someone I trusted or was too young to fully understand them.

Satan is the worst! He's the worst because he (lowercase *h* intended) had the audacity to make me feel worthless for every single thing I had ever done or that was done to me. This aspect of confessing was the most eye-opening and educational part of kicking the can.

When we got back to the driveway, President Bott asked again, "Is that everything?" I assured him it was, and then he said words that saturated my soul with joy: "You are forgiven. Now get to work!"

At that very moment, I felt an undeniable warm, peaceful feeling cover me from my head to my toes. I knew I had been forgiven and had just needed this last step.

On that day during my mission, I was covered. On that day, I was healed. I had my own Day of Atonement and, to be honest, I've had many others since, all of which qualify me to have a place and to sit down with the Husband and the elders of the land. While ten-year-old Tammy's plan seemed simple and perfect, she never imagined repenting would be such a crucial, important, and beautiful part of her life. She now understands that her life plan is less about having a famous husband and is really about the Atonement of Jesus Christ and keeping covenants. End of plan.

NOTES

24.

She maketh fine linen, and selleth it; and delivereth girdles unto the merchant.

‏24. סָדִין עָשְׂתָה וַתִּמְכֹּר וַחֲגוֹר נָתְנָה לַכְּנַעֲנִי:

GROWING UP, MY PARENTS DID an excellent job teaching my siblings and me the importance of work. For many of our financial requests, their response was, "Well, figure it out." And so we did. We have worked almost any job there is to work. You name it, and an Uzelac has probably done it. Janitorial? Yup. Fireworks stand? Check. Strawberry picking in the hot and humid Missouri summer? You bet. Hang, mud, and tape drywall? Why not? Professional cake decorating? Oh, we've got one of those. Interior design? We've got that too. And while we're at it, let's go ahead and include every fast-food place or dining establishment on the list. My siblings and I are all scrappers and proud of it. We will find a way to make a buck. So, when I taught this verse in seminary, it was easy for me to interpret what it meant. I told my students, "The virtuous woman works hard and, now here, she has a side gig." But I've since learned that a hopeful Old Testament girl's interpretation of this verse would be much different.

The combination of the words *linen* and *girdles* in this verse would stir up strong emotions for any young woman living during biblical times who anxiously anticipated the day she would be married. *Fine linen* and a *girdle* are two of the items she would wear on her wedding day.[173] In verse 23, the virtuous woman, as a bride, is dressed in her wedding garments, and she is anxiously awaiting her Bridegroom—Jesus Christ.

She maketh fine linen, and selleth it

This verse begins with the word סָדִין (*sadin*), which is a linen wrap or garment.[174] This could be referring to an outer wrapping worn as a luxury item[175] that was worn as part of a woman's wedding clothes. On her wedding day, the first thing that she would put on is a fine linen robe.[176] Donald W. Parry, a professor of the Hebrew Bible in the Department of Asian and Near Eastern Languages at Brigham Young University, explains the reason for this: "The bridal clothing . . . was of white linen, symbolic of righteousness and purity."[177] Once the young woman was dressed in a linen robe, she would then be ready to *selleth it*.

The word *selleth* can be translated as "to sell oneself or sell a daughter in marriage."[178] The bride's price has already been paid, and the wedding linen is prepared so she can be sold or offer herself as a covenant daughter in marriage to the symbolic merchant, the one who bought her with a price (see 1 Corinthians 6:20, 7:23). Wearing the linen wrap, she will next tie on girdles as she waits for the bridegroom, to whom she will ceremoniously *deliver the girdles*.

and delivereth girdles

The *girdle* in this verse is "a belt, or sash,"[179] and its symbolism is powerful. The Old Testament teaches us that as part of the sacred temple vestments worn by a priest, a girdle or sash was wrapped around the wearer several times as a reminder of being bound to the Lord and His covenants. Scholars believe that "the girdle was traditionally wrapped around the chest as a symbolic reminder to the wearer that the Atonement cleanses them of sinful thoughts of the heart, [for it atones] where it is [worn]."[180] It signifies that, as a bride of God (one of His people), the wearer is bound to the Lord through covenants. The same holds true for the virtuous woman. The girdle is another significant part of her bridal clothing.

Often the girdles were embroidered, and after putting on the linen robe, a woman would take two girdles and wrap herself twice. One would be tied tightly around her chest, the other around her waist.[181] Both symbolized commitment, purity, and faithfulness.[182] Before consummating the marriage, the bride would enter the wedding tent, untie the girdles, and *deliver* them to the groom. This was a sign to her husband of her virginity, fidelity, and commitment to him.[183] Symbolically, the woman's girdle represents the covenants she has kept and her faithfulness and commitment to the Lord. While on a trip with my friend Tamu, I saw what it truly meant to have this level of commitment.

My friend Tamu is married and has many kids who live or have lived in her home. She and her husband, Keith, have five biological children. They have also raised Tamu's six siblings and have welcomed in *a lot* of friends who have needed a place to stay. She has even offered up her "Prophet and Jesus room"—you know, that one room in the house that is the cleanest and nicest that is reserved for special guests.

In 2019, Tamu and I were part of the Time Out for Women tour with several other people. While on this trip, I imagined Tamu being able to take a nice break. I assumed she would enjoy the peace and quiet and being able to sleep in. So, when Sunday came, a few of us decided to meet down in the lobby and go to church together. As we were about to leave, Tamu jumped out of the elevator dressed to the nines, ready to get her worship on (as she would say).

I looked at her and said, "Tamu! I thought you would take this morning to sleep in and enjoy your peace and rest."

Tamu replied, "Girl, I ain't sleepin' in on Jesus. I'll sleep in on my husband and my kids, but not Jesus. Let's go to church!"

Her example and exuberance were proof of her fidelity and commitment to Christ. Tamu loves Jesus. You know she does because she talks about him all the time. Jesus is a part of her everyday vocabulary. She gives Him credit for everything. Tamu's girdles are wrapped tight, and she is waiting for the day when she will unwrap them and deliver them *unto the merchant.*

unto the merchant

Christ is the merchant who, through the marriage covenant, paid for and now owns the bride. He has paid the price, and as a result, to Him, she is *segullah*. In Exodus 19:5, the Lord tells the children of Israel that if they commit to obey His voice and keep His covenant, they will be a segullah, or "peculiar treasure" unto Him. Other translations for this term include "valued property"[184] or "the Lord's own special people or treasure."[185] You are segullah to the Lord; you are special to Him. You are His treasure (Psalms 135:4). You are loved! The single most important belief in a woman's life is that her husband, metaphorically the Lord and Savior Jesus Christ, loves and adores her. And not just because He loves everyone, but because He specifically and individually knows her and loves her. You are His favorite! Elder Jeffrey R. Holland affirmed, "No one of us is less treasured or cherished of God than another . . . He loves each of us— insecurities, anxieties, self-image and all."[186]

We are His pearl of great price. We are symbolically wearing linen and are wrapped in girdles, "prepared as a Bride adorned for her husband" (Revelation 21:1–2). We will "go forth to meet the Bridegroom" (D&C 133:10), and as His bride, we will deliver ourselves to Him. Our symbolic linen and girdles represent all the work we have done and the disciples we have become. Those items will show that a virtuous woman doesn't need a side gig; she just serves Jesus.

NOTES

25.

Strength and honour are her clothing; and she shall rejoice in time to come.

25. עֹז־וְהָדָר לְבוּשָׁהּ וַתִּשְׂחַק לְיוֹם אַחֲרוֹן׃

In September 2017, the current Young Women General Presidency recorded an interview/Q&A called "How to Help Young Women Feel Valued and Needed in the Church." There are about 29,500 views for this video on YouTube, and I'm almost certain that about half of them are mine! I have watched it so many times. It is incredible. These three amazing women addressed a pressing issue among young women in the Church today.

Sister Bonnie L. Oscarson explained that the inspiration for this Q&A came from a meeting she attended. At the meeting, leaders of the Church were talking about the visibility of young men and their participation in ordinances of the priesthood on a weekly basis, specifically in sacrament meetings. A man turned to her and asked, "What do the young women of the Church have that makes them know that they are important too?" She said this question gave her pause and she didn't have an immediate answer. She told about her experiences traveling and meeting with Young Women leaders and asking them,

"How do your young women see themselves as a part of the work of the priesthood?" The answer was always the same: "We teach our young women to support the priesthood."[187] This opened the conversation for Sister Oscarson, Sister McConkie, and Sister Marriott to teach us about young women and the priesthood power they hold.

Verse 25 answers the very question that was asked of Sister Oscarson. And we will see, as Sister Neill F. Marriott said in that interview (quoting President Oaks), "*The* priesthood is not *the* men of the Church. Priesthood is the power of God and we *all* work with that power."[188] In this verse, that power is represented by the virtuous woman's clothing. It can't be bought or made, it can only be obtained through covenants.

Strength and honour are her clothing

In 1838, another important Q&A happened. A man by the name of Elias Higbee asked Joseph Smith to explain the command in Isaiah 52:1 to "put on thy strength, O Zion." The Lord revealed to Joseph Smith that "to put on her strength is to put on the authority of the priesthood, which she, Zion, has a right to by lineage; also to return to that power which she had lost" (D&C 113:7–8). Isaiah 52:1 is repeated three other times in the Book of Mormon, reminding us how significant and important it is to "put on thy strength," which is the priesthood power (2 Nephi 8:24; 3 Nephi 20:36; Moroni 10:31). The word עֹז (*oz*) begins verse 25 and means "strength." The same word is used in scriptures from Isaiah and the Book of Mormon.[189] The word *honour*, spelled *honor* in American

English, can also mean "majesty,"[190] and it is this majesty coupled with strength that the Lord clothes Himself in. Psalm 93:1 describes the Lord as being "clothed with majesty" and "clothed with strength." His clothing is a symbol of His power, the priesthood power that He has given all women and men to accomplish His work here on earth.

Today, every member of The Church of Jesus Christ of Latter-day Saints has access to putting on this strength or power. President Russell M. Nelson wants every woman and man to know that they adorn themselves with strength and honor by entering into covenants:

> Every woman and every man who makes covenants with God and keeps those covenants, and who participates worthily in priesthood ordinances, has direct access to the power of God. Those who are endowed in the house of the Lord receive a gift of God's priesthood power by virtue of their covenant, along with a gift of knowledge to know how to draw upon that power. The heavens are just as open to women who are endowed with God's power flowing from their priesthood covenants as they are to men who bear the priesthood. I pray that truth will register upon each of your hearts because I believe it will change your life. Sisters, you have the right to draw liberally upon the Savior's power to help your family and others you love.[191]

Covenant-keeping women are endowed with power, priesthood power. Barbara Morgan Gardner's book *The Priesthood Power of Women: In the Temple, Church, and Family* does an incomparable job of explaining women and the priesthood. Throughout her book, she teaches the principle that the priesthood is not the men of the Church but rather the priesthood is God's power given to His children to accomplish His purposes here on earth. She points out that God's power looks different for His daughters than for His sons. Quoting prophets and apostles, Gardner describes what it looks like for women:

> What kind of power do women have? Women who make and keep covenants in the temple have "the power of enlightenment, of testimony, and of understanding." They can pray, receiving guidance from the Lord at an even greater level because of the endowment they have received in the temple. Women have the "power [to] thwart the forces of evil," or, in other words, to contend and win against the power of Satan in their own lives, in their homes, or while they travel. They have the "power to use [their] gifts and capabilities with greater intelligence and increased effectiveness" than they would have otherwise been able to. Women have the "power to overcome the sins of the world," are "better qualified to

teach," and can protect and "strengthen their earthly families."[192]

This power and the use of the priesthood began with Eve in the Garden of Eden. According to Jewish tradition, Adam and Eve "were often apart in the Garden engaged in separate tasks to which each was best fitted."[193] There was neither patriarchy nor matriarchy in the garden; the two supported each other.[194] Together they worked to accomplish the Lord's purposes, each bringing their gifts and talents combined with the power of the priesthood. Eve was a helpmeet to her husband. Though helpmeet is spelled as one word in modern spelling, in Genesis 2:18 and in Hebrew, it is two separate words. The words *help* and *meet* are probably two of my favorite Hebrew words. The first word, *help*, is עזר (*ezer*) and means to help and is from the root word for "succor," meaning to run to give aid or help. The second part of the word is *meet*, which is כנגדו (*k'enegdo*), and according to late rabbinical commentaries, means "like or as his equal."[195]

Eve was made as an equal to Adam, not as subservient or inferior to him. For centuries and eons of time, Satan has enjoyed twisting and distorting the meaning of this verse, which has unfortunately slowed and almost eradicated women's role in this world. Sister Jean B. Bingham said, "Satan incites comparison as a tool to create feelings of being superior or inferior, hiding the eternal truth that men's and women's innate differences are God given and equally valued. . . . Our roles are complementary rather than competitive."[196] Eve and

Adam needed the combined power from each of their gifts, as well as the priesthood, to be successful.

It's amazing to think that one of the very first elements of Christ's original Church to be restored was the authority of the priesthood of God. Sister Bingham perfectly pointed out that "as the restoration continued to unfold, men and women began to realize the importance and potential of working as partners, authorized and directed in this sacred labor by Him."[197] A unique and poignant example of this was seen in one of the last interactions Emma had with her husband, Joseph.

As a covenant woman, Emma Hale Smith's life with her husband was met with persecution, calumny, oppression, and disdain. It was also met with heartache. In the first five years of their marriage, they lost four babies. Of her eleven children, she buried six in all. Inundated with arrests and time spent in jail, on June 24, 1844, Joseph was once again faced with the possibility of incarceration. To meet the demands of persecutors, including Thomas Ford, the governor of Illinois, Joseph left for what would be his last incarceration, spent in Carthage Jail. Before he left, Emma asked him for a blessing. Joseph told Emma to write out the best blessing she could think of and he would sign it.[198] Pregnant at the time with their eleventh child, Emma wrote out her blessing:

> First of all that I would crave as the richest of heaven's blessings would be wisdom from my Heavenly Father bestowed daily, so that whatever I might do or say, I could not look back

at the close of the day with regret, nor neglect the performance of any act that would bring a blessing. I desire the Spirit of God to know and understand myself, that I desire a fruitful, active mind, that I may be able to comprehend the designs of God, when revealed through his servants without doubting. I desire a spirit of discernment, which is one of the promised blessings of the Holy Ghost. I particularly desire wisdom to bring up all the children that are, or may be committed to my charge, in such a manner that they will be useful ornaments in the Kingdom of God, and in a coming day arise up and call me blessed. I desire prudence that I may not through ambition abuse my body and cause it to become prematurely old and care-worn, but that I may wear a cheerful countenance, live to perform all the work that [I] covenanted to perform in the spirit-world and be a blessing to all who may in any wise need aught at my hands. I desire with all my heart to honor and respect my husband as my head, ever to live in his confidence and by acting in unison with him retain the place which God has given me by his side, and I ask my Heavenly Father that through humility, I may be enabled to overcome the curse which was pronounced upon the daughters of Eve. I desire to see that I may rejoice with them in the blessings which God has in store for all who are willing to be obedient to his requirements. Finally, I desire that whatever may be my lot through life I may be enabled to acknowledge the hand of God in all things.[199]

This is the priesthood in action. Emma's requests were motivated by her power, faith, covenants, and conviction in Christ. *The* priesthood is *the* women and men of the church. Emma's life was complicated and not met without conflict, but she was clothed in strength and honor, and she has certainly rejoiced in time to come.

and she shall rejoice in time to come

The phrase "in time to come" can refer to either a generic future time or a specific time to come.[200] The Septuagint translates this verse as, "She rejoices in the last days (ἐν ἡμέραις ἐσχάταις)."[201] This "time to come" of verse 25 is now. In the Q&A with Joseph Smith and Elias Higbee, the Lord revealed that Isaiah 52:1 also had reference to "those whom God should call in the *last days*, who should hold the power of the priesthood to bring again Zion, and the redemption of Israel" (D&C 113:8; emphasis added). This is referring to the preparatory work to be done before the Second Coming. Virtuous women are clothed in the priesthood, and "as covenant-keeping women, we are commissioned to save souls and to be a part of the gathering of Israel. . . . All who fully enter into covenants with the Lord . . . are taking part in the gathering of the House of Israel."[202]

Women and men can work together to accomplish the Lord's purposes by using their individual gifts and talents in the last days. President Nelson told us what this can look like:

> When we speak of gathering Israel on both sides of the veil, we are referring, of course, to missionary, temple, and family history work. We are also referring to building faith and testimony in the hearts of those with whom we live, work, and serve. Anytime we do anything that helps anyone—on either side of the veil—to make and keep their covenants with God, we are helping to gather Israel.[203]

We live in the last days, the days leading up to the Second Coming of our Lord and Savior Jesus Christ. He is coming. Sister Bingham asked if we are ready for the Second Coming of Christ. Are we willing to let God prevail in our lives? Are we ready to overcome cultural biases, work together, learn to value everyone's unique contributions, and increase the effectiveness with which we fulfill our divine roles?[204] This is such an exciting time that we live in; of course we will rejoice! We rejoice as we participate in the gathering of Israel. We rejoice in the priesthood that is ours to help us in these last days, looking to the future cheerfully. We rejoice in being a help meet with others to accomplish the Lord's purposes. Sister

Bingham promised that if we can do this, "we will feel greater joy than we have ever experienced."

As we choose to let God prevail in our lives, we will rejoice when He comes again because we will be "adorned as a bride . . . clothed upon with robes of righteousness and salvation . . . and . . . shout aloud for joy" (see D&C 109:74–80). Like Eve and Adam and Emma and Joseph, we all need each other, and this is the pattern given to us by the Lord. Single, married, widowed, divorced, male or female, all of us can be clothed in strength and honor through our covenants, blessing the lives of God's children on either side of the veil. All of us play an important role in the work of the priesthood—all of us. And when women are taught that *strength and honour* are their clothing, they too will begin to see and believe how much God needs them and will understand the specific work He needs them to do.

NOTES

HER ATTRIBUTES—
VERSES 26–30

26.

She openeth her mouth with wisdom; and in her tongue is the law of kindness.

26. פִּיהָ פָּתְחָה בְחָכְמָה וְתוֹרַת־חֶסֶד עַל־לְשׁוֹנָהּ:

I HAVE KNOWN HALEY SINCE she was a little girl. She is the niece of my two dearest friends (who are sisters), and to know Haley is to love her. I got to watch her grow up and become an amazing woman. When Haley went to college, she was the quintessential college co-ed. With her blonde hair and blue eyes, she bounced onto campus ready to take on the world. She was so excited to finally be on her own. She enrolled as a full-time student. She was selected to join a popular sorority. She had so many friends and dated *a lot*! In 2020, as I was preparing to schedule guests for the Sunday on Monday podcast, her name came to my mind, and I knew she needed to be a guest. I thought I knew her story, but that day on the show, she opened up and taught me about the meaning of verse 26 in a way that I will never forget.

First, though, we need to explore the translation of the words in this verse. To some, it may seem obvious. To quote Thumper from *Bambi*, "If ya can't say somethin' nice, don't say nuffin' at all," or put more simply, "Don't be a jerk." But in this verse, wisdom coupled with kindness will show a powerful connection between covenants and Christ. Verse 26 begins our last quintet, which describes the attributes of the virtuous woman. These verses don't add further attributes to the ones we have already read about; they summarize who the virtuous woman is and what has enabled her to accomplish all that she has up to this point in the proverb. And here in verse 26, we learn that opening our mouths with wisdom and having on our tongues the "law of kindness" guides us to become more Christlike.

She openeth her mouth with wisdom

This verse begins with the word פִּיהָ(*peh*), which is "mouth, or to speak."[205] The virtuous woman opens her mouth and speaks with wisdom. No college course, diploma, fifteen-step program, or self-help group can teach this type of wisdom. This wisdom has been accumulated over the course of the last sixteen verses that we have studied. In D&C 45:57, the Lord defines the wise as those who "have received the truth, and have taken the Holy Spirit for their guide, and have not been deceived." Women who speak wisdom are essential and instrumental to our Heavenly Father and His work. President Russell M. Nelson encouraged women to speak wisdom when he said, "We, your brethren, need your strength, your conversion, your conviction . . . your wisdom, and your voices. The kingdom of God is not and cannot be complete without women who make sacred covenants and then keep them, women who can speak with the power and authority of

God."[206] Today, virtuous women are strengthening the world's faith in Jesus Christ, not only through their wisdom, but also through the law of kindness.

and in her tongue is the law of kindness

So, how kind do we have to be and what does this look like in everyday life? One commentary states this part of the verse means the virtuous woman "has the ready tact which takes advantage of every opportunity to render the lives of others happier."[207] Everything we have studied so far in Proverbs 31 is evidence of this definition. But the phrase *law of kindness* is what makes this verse so striking.

The *law* spoken of in this verse is *torah*. This is not the same meaning as *Torah*, which is "the Law," or the first five books of Moses. This lowercase *torah* means "kind instruction, wise words of a woman or mother."[208] As interpreted by some, this means the virtuous woman "opens her mouth with wisdom and either teaches about kindness, or that it is with kindness that she gives the instruction."[209] Here she does both, given the translation for the word *kindness*.

The Hebrew word for *kindness* used in this verse is חסד (*hesed*) and goes beyond the meaning of being nice. This word is difficult to translate because of the intense emotion behind its meaning. It can mean up to fifteen different terms and is most synonymous with mercy, kindness, loyalty, and loving-kindness. It refers to a deeply powerful loving-kindness that the Father feels for His children. It is an unwavering love so strong that He is willing to condescend to the needs of His creatures, helping us in our neediest and most miserable of moments. It can even redeem us from our enemies and our troubles.[210] Even though hesed is predominantly a divine action, some argue that even we can have hesed, suggesting that it is a characteristic common to both the nature of man and his relationship to the nature of God.[211] This is seen in the book of Ruth, and according to some Jewish sources, the purpose of her story is to teach us about hesed.[212]

The word *hesed* is used three times in the story of Ruth. First: After the death of Naomi's husband and sons, Naomi tells her daughters-in-law to go back to their mothers' homes and then gives them a blessing, saying, "The Lord deal kindly [hesed] with you, as ye have dealt with the dead, and with me" (Ruth 1:8). Their implied acts of hesed (kindness) toward Naomi qualified them for the hesed of the Lord.

Second: After Ruth gleans from the field of Boaz, she returns to Naomi and tells her all about him and the compassion he had on her. Naomi is thrilled and says to Ruth, "Blessed be he of the Lord, who hath not left off his kindness [hesed] to the living and to the dead" (Ruth 2:20). While Boaz imparted hesed to Ruth, Naomi knew it was God who deserved the credit. These virtuous women were not forgotten and were blessed with His hesed.

Third: After Ruth asks Boaz to marry her, he praises her for her kindness. In the same verse shared above, Naomi also says of Boaz, "The man is near of kin unto us, one of our next kinsmen" (Ruth 2:20). A near kinsman had the legal right to purchase the land of a deceased relative, marry his widow, and have children with her. Naomi pointed out to Ruth that Boaz could marry her and save them both. At this time, there was a certain degree of shame that came with being a widow. A widow could not work or provide for herself, she would live a life of poverty, she had no one to protect her, and she would be at a severe social and economic disadvantage. Isaiah references these circumstances when he mentions the "reproach of thy widowhood" (Isaiah 54:4). Ruth and Naomi together were a double dose of reproach, and they needed help. As the story goes, Ruth actually ends up proposing to Boaz, and he kindly responds to her request, "Blessed be thou of the Lord, my daughter: for thou hast shewed more kindness [done more hesed] in the latter end than at the beginning, inasmuch as thou followedst not young men, whether poor or rich" (Ruth 3:10).[213] What Boaz is saying is, "Wow! I am blessing you for the hesed you have shown to Naomi and how willing you are to follow the laws of God and build up your deceased husband's name and memory by marrying me, an old man, when you could have married anyone else who was younger." Marrying anyone else outside of the family would have only benefitted Ruth and left Naomi out in the cold. But what mattered to Ruth was the redemptive qualities of Boaz (the kinsman) for both her *and* Naomi.

After Boaz and Ruth were married, the women of the city said to Naomi, "Blessed be the Lord, which hath not left thee this day without a kinsman [redeemer], that his name may be famous in Israel" (Ruth 4:14). Boaz's act of redemption saved Ruth and Naomi from the reproach of their widowhood and, in time, Christ was born as Boaz's descendant (refer back to chart on page 29).

The examples of hesed in the story of Ruth are particularly inspiring to all of God's children. Religious scholar Kerry Muhlestein tells us, "We cannot read of [Ruth's] devotion without hoping that we will always have a Ruth in our lives, and simultaneously aspiring to be a Ruth for others." He then sums up the story of Ruth and the benefits of hesed by saying: "In a manner of speaking, Ruth's redemption is our own. From Ruth we can better understand the Savior, his covenants with us, the rest God has in store for us, and Christ's glorious redeeming power."[214] Is there someone that comes to mind that has been a Ruth for you in your life? Haley had a Ruth.

I invited Haley to the Sunday on Monday podcast to discuss 2 Nephi 31–33, which teaches about the Holy Ghost, believing in Christ, and enduring to the end. During the last segment of the episode, we concluded with reading 2 Nephi 33:10:

> And now, my beloved brethren, and also Jew, and all ye ends of the earth, hearken unto these words and believe in Christ; and if ye believe not in these words believe in Christ. And if ye shall believe in Christ ye will believe in these words, for they are the words of Christ, and he hath given them unto me; and they teach all men that they should do good.

Then I asked Haley, "How has believing in Christ helped you endure to the end?" Haley's response taught me everything

I needed to know about the meaning of Proverbs 31:26. Here is her response:

> When you read scriptures like this, I feel like you go back to those hard times in your life and those hard times help you to grow. One hard time I think of, which has turned into such a blessing for me, is when I was young and in college, and just living the best life, not married, and then I found out I was pregnant.
>
> I think back on that specific day, not seeing any light. At the time I didn't have a strong testimony, and I didn't have the Holy Ghost with me or so I thought. But looking back, I did have the Holy Ghost with me because something came over me, and I believe it was the Spirit saying, "Text your mom." I instantly thought "No way! Over my dead body was I ever going to tell my mom!" but at that time and in that moment, I knew what I needed to do. So I texted my mom and said, "I need you." Just three little words and she immediately replied, "I'm on my way!"
>
> My mom didn't ask any questions, she just got in her car and drove. She lived about twenty minutes away, and when she came into my apartment, I said, "I'm pregnant.

And I don't know what I'm going to do. I don't want a baby right now, and I don't know what my options are." She looked at me and without hesitation said, "Whatever you decide to do I will support you and I will be there for you." At that moment, I believed that it was Christ speaking to me. That wasn't my mom. And she will even say looking back on that moment, something came over her to give her those words to say. That was such a hard time, obviously, and a hard day for all of us, but to hear those words from her it felt like it was the Spirit hugging me in that moment. And those words she spoke were the words of Christ to me, and everything was going to be fine. I mean from that time on obviously it was really hard, and now it is the biggest blessing in my life. It has really shaped who I am today and also my family. I had this beautiful daughter, I got married, and then we were sealed. That was a really big turning point for me that started my journey to endure to the end. And I'm still enduring.[215]

We had spent much of that episode talking about the Holy Ghost and what the Holy Ghost can do for us, and then unexpectedly, Haley's story became an incredible example of what hesed looked like in her neediest and possibly most miserable moment. Haley's virtuous mother showed her daughter a divine kindness that was powerful and unwavering. Her mother spoke wisdom and was the "law of kindness" for her daughter that day. She spoke the words of Christ. Her mom was able to say what needed to be said, and it comforted Haley when she needed to be comforted. In that moment, she was a full fruition of President M. Russell Ballard's statement that "the power of a converted woman's voice is immeasurable."[216]

Verse 26 is about a virtuous woman's wisdom testifying of her divine Redeemer through words and the law of hesed. We can be a Ruth for others, using words that can heal, inspire, cheer, comfort, teach, testify, and bless. Like Ruth and Haley's mom, women today are opening their mouths with wisdom and kindness and are building up His kingdom. Their lives and words are a confession of Christ, testifying of their faith in and devotion to Him.[217]

NOTES

27.

She looketh well to the ways of her household, and eateth not the bread of idleness.

27. צוֹפִיָּה הֲלִיכוֹת בֵּיתָהּ וְלֶחֶם עַצְלוּת לֹא תֹאכֵל:

"HAND ME YOUR PHONE." THIS simple request of Julie to her son led her down a path that she never wanted to step foot on. She had recently learned how to do an advanced search on a cell phone to check the browsing history. Out of curiosity, one random afternoon, she said, "Hand me your phone," to her sixteen-year-old son. She searched and found a history that was replete with pornography. Her heart dropped, and immediately, she began to shake. Her husband was in the bedroom, and with the phone still in her hand, she casually got up, walked into their room and shut the door. She fell on the bed and, through the heartbroken tears of a mother, she cried out, "Our son is looking at pornography." It is a journey that no parent, spouse, or friend wants to begin and yet, one that is familiar to many. From that moment on, Julie's decision to help her son and the future of her family is what verse 27 is all about.

Verse 27 is not implying that a virtuous woman be busier, stay up later, get up earlier, or work harder than she is already;

this verse simply describes what she is doing and how she gets it all done. In actuality, verse 27 is answering the call given from President Russell M. Nelson, "We need women who are devoted to shepherding God's children along the covenant path toward exaltation."[218]

She looketh well to the ways of her household

The opening words of this verse are *looketh well*, written in Hebrew as צוֹפִיָּה (*tsophiah*), which means "to keep the watch, look out, a watchman."[219] The phrase *to the ways of her household* is actually translated as "watching the doings of her household, or traveling company."[220] That is exactly what my friend Julie had done. She was very aware of the responsibility she had to stand as a *watchwoman over her household*, and she acted. Ezekiel, the Old Testament prophet and watchman, taught that being a successful watchman would "deliver his soul," but if the watchman failed in his duty, the Lord said He will "require at the watchman's hand" (Ezekiel 33:5–6). Traditionally, a watchman was set on a tower or wall to watch for the safety of the people. The responsibilities of a watchman were heavy:

- They were to watch for the enemy and then warn everyone (Ezekiel 33:8–9, 14, 16).
- The watchman had to stay awake and would face execution if he failed to warn the city when the enemy appeared.
- Such a watchman was in jeopardy always: the enemy sought to destroy him to keep him from raising the

warning and, if he did not raise the warning when it was needed, his life was in jeopardy at the hands of those he was responsible to warn.[221]

As a watchwoman, the virtuous woman is similar to the Father: "As Almighty God, from His lofty watch-tower in heaven, she observes all the minutest details of the manifold work that is going on in the busy hive of earth, so does she from her exalted position in which He has placed her, as mistress of the family, and as responsible to Him, she observes the ways of her household."[222] Over the years, I have watched Julie carefully and vigilantly watch over her family, feeling a deep sense of responsibility for her children and anyone else in her household that might be lost. This effort requires a particular type of action, and there is very little room to eat the bread of idleness.

and eateth not the bread of idleness

As Latter-day Saints, we are very familiar with the concept of working hard and the unfortunate results of being idle: "And the idler shall not have place in the church, except he repent and mend his ways" (D&C 75:29). We are even commanded not to be idle: "Wherefore, I give unto them a commandment, thus: Thou shalt not idle away thy time" (D&C 60:13). It was an "abundance of idleness" that first led to the downfall of Sodom and Gomorrah (Ezekiel 16:49). But this part of the verse isn't asking us to do more, it is simply asking us to keep doing what we are doing. As the virtuous woman watches over her household, the next part of the verse is clear; as a covenant-keeping woman, she doesn't have time to be idle or "without labor."[223] Virtuous women are hard workers. Their lives are proof that keeping God's covenants is insurance from idleness; keeping covenants requires work. This does not imply that we should become frenetic overachievers constantly in motion. We are counseled to not run faster than we have strength (see D&C 10:4; Mosiah 4:27), and Elder Dieter F. Uchtdorf counseled us that we would do well to "slow down a little, proceed at the optimum speed for our circumstances, focus on the significant, lift up our eyes, and truly see the things that matter most."[224] I love that Elder Uchtdorf included in his statement, "proceed at the optimum speed for our circumstances." My friend Holly taught me a powerful lesson about this statement.

Holly and her husband are the parents of twenty-five children. That's right. Twenty-five. I know, it blew my mind the first time I heard her say that. In 1990, Holly's husband was watching the television program *20/20* when host Barbara Walters highlighted the story about orphaned children in Romania. Immediately Holly's husband told her to come in and watch. As she learned of the desperate circumstances of these children, Holly had a noticeably clear and spiritual impression that she was to go to Romania and adopt. Within a few short weeks, she was there and adopting two little girls. Over the course of thirty years, Holly and her husband have had four biological children, and they have adopted 20 more, while also raising a grandchild.

Some of the children that Holly and her husband have adopted are termed "hard to place," meaning that they are older or suffer with physical and/or mental disabilities. Holly has spent most of her life mothering and has been a hard worker for a really long time. When I first met her, I asked her how she did it. She told of being so busy with so many little kids at home that she could scarcely shower. "I could barely shave my legs. Maybe I could do one and then a week later do the other one." I asked Holly to be a guest on the Sunday on Monday podcast, and it just so happened that we were discussing Doctrine and Covenants 10:4, which reads, "Do not run faster or labor more than you have strength and means provided to enable you to translate; but be diligent unto the end." Joseph Smith received this revelation after having the plates and Urim and Thumim returned to him following the incident of losing 116 pages of the Book of Mormon manuscript. He was anxious to get back to the work of translating the plates. His wife, Emma, was recovering from a traumatic childbirth (where she almost died) and the grief of losing the child. Joseph was ready to translate, but he needed a scribe and needed to provide for his family. The Lord fittingly instructed Joseph to not run faster or labor more than he had strength.

Discussing Doctrine and Covenants 10:4 with Holly taught me an important lesson about running versus being idle. I asked Holly to read the verse out loud, and she immediately let out a short laugh. After she read the verse, I asked her why she laughed. She said:

> People are always using this verse to tell me to slow down and that I don't need to do as much as I am doing. I think the idea for every-one is to pace yourself, but don't be afraid to

run as fast as you DO have strength. I think
we sometimes get into trouble when we are
looking at people running their own race and
think. "My race should look like theirs." If
you're called to it great, but if you're not then
just run your own race. I literally prayed for
God to give me the strength and He did. I
prayed to get by on less sleep and He gave that
to me. But, that's my race.

As a result of this philosophy, Holly and her husband,
in *their* circumstances, have been able to fulfill the last part
of Elder Uchtdorf's counsel to "focus on the significant, lift
up our eyes, and truly see the things that matter most." That
statement right there is how I would define the message of
verse 27. It isn't asking us to do more, just to do well with what
we have been given. As watchmen on their tower, Holly and
her husband have looked well to the ways of their household
and have not eaten the bread of idleness . . . in their own way.

Proverbs 31:27 is not implying that a virtuous woman
should be doing something new or more of what she is already
doing. Verse 27 is a reminder that the virtuous woman has
spent the last seventeen verses focused on the things that matter
most. She has spent the last seventeen verses building a spiritual
fortress and preparing to warn others of the enemy who, by the
way, is "as a roaring lion, [walking] about, seeking whom he
may devour" (1 Peter 5:8). Julie was not about to let that lion
consume her child. She utilized every resource available to her.

With the help of their bishop, a therapist, rules, fasting, and countless prayers, Julie, her husband, and their son were able to manage the damaging and painful effects of pornography.

Julie's and Holly's testimonies of the gospel, along with their covenantal membership in The Church of Jesus Christ of Latter-day Saints, serve as their "personal fortresses of protection surrounding us and shielding us from the power of the evil one."[225] Being a watchman is personal. 1 Peter 5:8 teaches us how we can prepare for that roaring lion preying upon us: "Be sober, be vigilant." This means to be self-controlled, calm, and watchful so that we may provide safety. This is what a virtuous woman does for her family and her household.

N O T E S

28.

Her children arise up, and call her blessed;
her husband also, and he praiseth her.
28. קָמוּ בָנֶיהָ וַיְאַשְּׁרוּהָ בַּעְלָהּ וַיְהַלְלָהּ׃

ONE OF THE TOPICS OF discussion that freely comes up in my
home is the Resurrection. Why? Well, if the Resurrection is
truly going to happen, then that means my two oldest girls
will get to see Mom-Michelle again. We've discussed this at
length, with all of the particulars and timing of everything . . .
as best we can. When I was newly married, early one morning
before the girls left to catch the bus for school, I was doing my
youngest stepdaughter's hair.

While I was parting her pigtails, she asked, "Mom, ya know
how we believe that Jesus is going to come again, and when He
does, everyone is getting resurrected?"

"Uh-huh" I replied, thinking, *We're talking about Jesus in
the morning. I'm such a good mom!*

She then asked, "Even Mom-Michelle, right?"

I gently answered, "Yup, even Mom-Michelle."

And then after a pause, because this seven-year-old was deep
in thought, she blurted out, "Yeah, well, when that happens
. . . you're gonna to have to sleep in the guest bedroom."

There's nothing like having a kid succinctly put you in your place . . . a very low place at that!

That conversation didn't exactly go the way I thought it would. In the words of Rodney Dangerfield, "I get no respect."

Roland Edmund Murphy, a Catholic priest and biblical scholar, made a rather humorous statement about verse 28: "It's about time that some reaction from the members of her family be expressed."[226] To the women who have raised children and are married, could there be a greater honor than to have your children call you *blessed* and for your husband to praise you? But for those women who have never experienced motherhood or marriage, this verse seems devastatingly unfair. Thankfully, verse 28 includes all women and reflects all who benefit from a virtuous woman's service, not just her family. And the best part of all is that the Lord is the One giving the praise.

Her children arise up

The Hebrew word for *children* used here, בֵּן (*ben*, pronounced "*bane*"), can also refer to a people or a nation. It is most commonly used in this way when referring to the children of Israel.[227] So, who are *her children* that this verse is referring to? In her famous talk, "Are We Not All Mothers?," Sheri L. Dew explained, "*We are all mothers in Israel . . .* our calling is to love and help lead the rising generation through the dangerous streets of mortality." She also said, "As daughters of our Heavenly Father, and as daughters of Eve, we are all mothers and we have always been mothers."[228] The *children* in this verse could either be referring to the virtuous woman's offspring or the children of Israel as a whole—those in her *household* and in the *vineyard* where she labors.

The Apostle John used this same idea throughout his three epistles. He repeatedly refers to the Saints and believers as his "little children," or "children" (1 John 2:1, 3:18, 4:4, 5:21; 2 John 1:1). His love and concern for the Saints ran so deeply that he couldn't help but call them *his children*. When he says, "I have no greater joy than to hear that my children walk in truth" (3 John 1:4), he is speaking to the believers, the Saints, not his own biological children.[229] These are the people he loved, served, watched over, worried about, and prayed over. The *children* of a virtuous woman are no different. They are the *household* she had been up with at *night*. Those to whom she gave a *portion*. The *poor* and *needy* whom she sat with in their disheartened and lonely places. They all make up the nation that will *arise up*, קוּם (*qum*),[230] and call her blessed.

and call her blessed; her husband also

The word *blessed* in this verse can also be translated as "pronounce happy."[231] The virtuous woman's children and husband arise up and call her happy. All that she has done and the labors she has performed make her happy. Here are a few scriptures that teach this:

- "He that hath mercy on the poor, happy is he" (Proverbs 14:21).
- "He that keepeth the law, happy is he" (Proverbs 29:18).
- "Happy is the man that feareth alway" (Proverbs 28:14).

- "Happy is that people, whose God is the Lord" (Psalm 144:15).

Keeping our covenants and doing the Lord's work will make us happy. Elder Von G. Keetch explained, "King Benjamin taught that those who keep the commands of God are 'blessed and happy . . . in all things, both temporal and spiritual' (Mosiah 2:41). God wants us to have joy."[232] Joy is our ultimate goal, and in the words of the Prophet Joseph Smith, "Happiness is the object and design of our existence; and will be the end thereof, if we pursue the path that leads to it; and this path is virtue, uprightness, faithfulness, holiness, and keeping all the commandments of God."[233]

Please, please, please understand that this in no way means that we must *always* be happy. It does mean that a virtuous woman knows that the *source* of happiness is her Savior. Emma Lou Thayne, the author of the beloved hymn "Where Can I Turn for Peace?," wrote that the verses were born out of a very troubled time in her life. At a BYU Women's Conference, she shared these comforting words regarding happiness and sorrow: "We do deserve to have the dignity of occasional depression; the right to be sad now and then; the quivering hope to be happy again—because surely the worst of times will become the best of times."[234] I've written these words in my scriptures as a reminder that it's OK to be sad. It's OK to be depressed. Our Savior, Jesus Christ, was familiar with not only the best of times but also the worst. He was "a man of sorrows, and acquainted with grief" (Isaiah 53:3). When He entered the Garden of Gethsemane, He "began to be sorrowful and very heavy . . . exceeding sorrowful, even unto death" (Matthew 26:37–38). The word *sorrowful* in Greek means deep grief, and the meaning of *very heavy* is depressed, dejected, or anguished. It is so comforting to know that the most perfect person to walk the earth and who is *the* source of happiness also knew what it felt like to be profoundly sad.

There is divine beauty and purpose in the Savior's willingness to feel depressed, dejected, and sad. How beautiful to think that Jesus gets it. He gets us. He understands exactly how we feel and has experienced everything we have experienced, which is why He can succor us. It is why He can run to us, offering aid and help in our darkest moments, the ones that seem void of any hope. I was discussing this miracle with a group of women when my friend Becky said, "Oh, I totally get it. I didn't understand Christ until I knew that He understood me." She went on to tell her story about her experience with depression. Her painful and seemingly hopeless experience made her wonder if she would ever know happiness again.

I was shocked by this new revelation about my friend. You see, Becky is happy. I am fairly certain that if you looked up the word *cheerleader* in the dictionary, her picture would be there. She was never an actual cheerleader in high school or anything like that, but she's the friend you call when you have an idea and need encouragement. You know she will cheer you on and champion your cause or dream, no matter how crazy it is. And her laugh! It's totally infectious! She is happiness, and being around her makes you happy too. She embodies verse 28—or at least she did until she lost her baby.

"There's no heartbeat." Becky looked over at her husband, whose eyes welled up with tears, and together they tried to process the words no expectant parent wants to hear. Becky was admitted to the hospital, and after three long, agonizing days, on Friday, January 3, 2003, she gave birth to a beautiful and lifeless baby boy. She and her husband held their son, trying to soak up a lifetime of "should haves" in this moment of impossibility. Becky remembers the surreal experience of leaving the hospital without a baby in her arms. Being wheeled through the maternity ward, she could hear the sound of newborn cries and felt the air around her filled with happiness and hope. Anger washed over her. She didn't get the prize for her hours of labor, and it wasn't fair. Going home empty-handed to a nursery that was no longer needed. It was devastating. She remembers the moment her milk came in and thinking, *Are you kidding me?! This is so unfair and another reminder that I didn't get what I felt was promised to me.*

When Becky was fifteen, she received her patriarchal blessing, which promised her that she would be a mother to *sons* and daughters who would grow up knowing Christ because of how she raised them. She thought, *Why would it say "sons" if my son was going to be taken away? Maybe God doesn't think I am good enough to have sons. Doesn't God trust me? Was I not good enough to fulfill that blessing?* Those thoughts played in her mind as if on repeat . . . over and over and over again. Her anger festered, and then depression settled into her heart and mind. For months, she refused contact from anyone. Her ward members rallied, offering help and meals, which she quickly dismissed, insisting she was "fine." She didn't sleep, didn't shower, didn't get dressed, didn't want to see anyone, and worst of all, didn't even want to be with her friends. After her husband left for work, she and her two-year-old daughter would sit in the basement, away from people, and watch TV all day long. Becky related the following story that changed everything for her:

> I wasn't "fine." People aren't fine. People are never going to be fine without Christ, who is the only one that can truly heal, and for one brief moment He healed my heart just enough to feel something I hadn't felt in months. One late afternoon, I heard my front door open. I could hear someone coming down my stairs. I looked up and saw my best friend Holly standing in the doorway. She commandingly said, "Enough. Enough! You are getting out of the house. You can't stay here any longer!" I was sitting there in my pajamas with a package of Oreo cookies and a 2-liter bottle of orange soda on my lap. I told Holly there was no way I was leaving my house, and besides, I was still in my pajamas. Holly said, "Oh good, because I'm in my pajamas, too. Now get up."
>
> Through my tears, I cried back, "But I don't need to buy anything."
>
> And Holly simply said, "Well neither do I, but staying down here is killing you, so let's go to the store."

The next thing I remember is pushing a grocery cart full of our little kids through the aisles and all of us eating popcorn and drinking blue raspberry slushies from the food court. Both of us in our pajamas with blue lips and slushie everywhere. I looked at us and realized how absurd it all was, and I just started laughing. It was the first time I had laughed in months. Laughing that day in the store was a turning point for me. I laughed. I felt happy. The emotion of laughter and happiness is what began my journey of believing, going to therapy, leaning on the Savior, and getting the help I needed, all of which were spiritually defining years for me. Looking back, I was the house in George Macdonald's analogy, quoted by C.S. Lewis:

"Imagine yourself as a living house. God comes in to rebuild that house. At first, perhaps, you can understand what He is doing. He is getting the drains right and stopping leaks in the roof and so on: you knew that those jobs needed doing and so you are not surprised. But presently He starts knocking the house about in a way that hurts abominably and does not seem to make sense. What on earth is He up to? The explanation is that He is building quite a different house from the one you thought of—throwing out a new wing here, putting on an extra floor there, running up towers, making courtyards. You thought you were going to be made into a decent little cottage: but He is building a palace. He intends to come and live in it Himself."[235]

I was that house. God took my sorrow, my loss, my depression, and used it to build me into something more than I could ever hope for myself. Losing my son was heartbreaking, but stopping the Lord from ripping down my walls and digging out my foundation would have been tragic. You know, as uncomfortable as it was, I would have my foundation dug out again. Jesus, as the general contractor and builder, was turning me into a mansion when I thought I was perfectly fine in a *tent*. And He is still doing that for me. Today, I am happy because I know who the source of my happiness is, and when I find myself in my basement with Oreos and orange soda, I know there is hope. And you know what? My three living children as well as the countless members of my "household" all know who Christ is because of my journey.

Elder Richard G. Scott taught, "True, enduring happiness, with the accompanying strength, courage, and capacity to overcome the greatest difficulties, will come as you center your life in Jesus Christ. . . . While there is no guarantee of overnight results, there is the assurance that, in the Lord's time, solutions will come, peace will prevail, and happiness will be yours."[236] In time, solutions came for Becky. She found peace and was happy again. Her best of times was magnified because she knew the worst. Allowing herself to be depressed ultimately created an intensity of happiness that she didn't know existed.

Our prophet, President Russell M. Nelson, familiar with some of the best of times, personally knew the worst. On the evening of February 12, 2005, his wife Dantzel suddenly slumped over and was gone due to a sudden heart attack. The prophet tried to resuscitate her but was unsuccessful. In his biography, he stated, "[I] sobbed and then sobbed some more. At one point, overcome with grief, [I] nearly screamed out loud."[237] And yet, with all of this sorrow he has experienced, he had this to say about being happy:

> Life is filled with detours and dead ends, trials and challenges of every kind. Each of us has likely had times when distress, anguish, and despair almost consumed us. Yet we are here to have joy? Yes! The answer is a resounding yes! But how is that possible? And what must we do to claim the joy that Heavenly Father has in store for us?

Saints can be happy under every circumstance. We can feel joy even while having a
bad day, a bad week, or even a bad year! My
dear brothers and sisters, the joy we feel has
little to do with the circumstances of our lives
and everything to do with the focus of our
lives.[238]

A virtuous woman knows the source of joy. She is a
committed disciple of Christ and, as a result, those who know
her call her blessed; the attribute of happiness is hers. She has
endured and persevered in the face of many storms. And now,
because of this, her *husband* will offer her His well-deserved
praise.

and he praiseth her

The virtuous woman's Husband, her Lord and Master, will
praise her. All that she has done, and all that she has become,
is worthy of the Savior's praise. But this is not limited to
a congratulatory type of praise. In this verse, the word for *to
praise* can also mean "glory."[239] She is counted among those
whom Peter spoke to when he said:

That the trial of your faith, being much more
precious than of gold that perisheth, though
it be tried with fire, might be found unto
praise and honour and *glory* at the appearing
of Jesus Christ: Whom having not seen, ye
love; in whom, though now ye see him not,
yet believing, ye rejoice with joy unspeakable

and full of *glory*: Receiving the end of your
faith, even the salvation of your souls. (1 Peter
1:7–9; emphasis added)

According to Peter's words, the Husband's praise and glory
will cause us to "rejoice with joy unspeakable" because we will
ultimately receive the salvation of our soul. Isaiah spoke of this
joy when he taught, "And as the bridegroom rejoiceth over the
bride, so shall thy God rejoice over thee" (Isaiah 62:5).

In this proverb, verses 28, 30, and 31 each end by saying
the virtuous woman is or will be praised. The reason this idea
of praise is repeated three times is to emphasize its importance.
This is called a climactic expression. It is a literary device used
in Hebrew to add power to the discourse through repetition,
connecting the ideas to a greater whole.[240] Repeating that "she
shall be praised" places importance on the overall outcome of
being a virtuous woman, which is found in verse 31.

Obviously, I don't know how it will all work out or what
bed I will sleep in, but what verse 28 offers me is the assurance
that as a virtuous woman, filled with God's power, I will be
praised. I will rejoice with joy unspeakable. I'm also a believer
in the words of Ugo Betti, an Italian judge, author, and
playwright: "To believe in God is to know that all the rules
will be fair, and that there will be wonderful surprises."[241]
Maybe the biggest surprise will be that Michelle and I will
share a room and Jim will have the guest bedroom.

NOTES

29.

Many daughters have done virtuously, but thou excellest them all.

‫29. רַבּוֹת בָּנוֹת עָשׂוּ חָיִל וְאַתְּ עָלִית עַל־כֻּלָּנָה:‬

ON MY KINDERGARTEN YEAR-END REPORT card, my teacher, Miss Crabtree, had two things to say about me: "Tammy is a good thinker. She sometimes seeks extra attention of others by leading."

Sure, I was a good thinker (thanks for the buffer comment, Miss Crabtree), but "seeks extra attention of others by leading"? Ummm, you bet I did! That's all I wanted growing up—attention! My main goal and objective was to be the leader and to be the best! I wanted to be the first, the smartest, the fastest, the toughest, THE BEST! Kindergarten Tammy would have read verse 29 and thought, *Game on! Let's do this!* I used to think this verse meant that the virtuous woman was THE BEST at being virtuous and that no one was better. But older and "more mature" Tammy reads it and thinks, *What qualified this woman to excel? Did she really do better than everyone else? How long did it take her? How much work did she have to do? Did she get to take a snack break?* I wonder, if many have done virtuously, could the only difference in each person's level of success be how long they worked at it? I think the Apostle James summed up this verse well when he said, "Behold, we count them happy which *endure*" (James 5:11; emphasis added).

Many daughters have done virtuously

This verse begins with רָב (*rab*), which means "many, an abundance or multitude."[242] A multitude of daughters have done virtuously, so why haven't they all excelled? The answer may be found in the parable of the ten virgins.

So, five were foolish and five were wise, but that doesn't necessarily mean that five were wicked and five were righteous. All ten virgins "took their lamps, and went forth to meet the bridegroom" (Matthew 25:1). They all had lamps and oil, meaning they knew who the bridegroom was, they were anxiously awaiting his arrival, and they were excited to be at the wedding feast. These women had most likely been taught throughout their lives that the bridegroom would come, and all ten of them were prepared with lamps that had oil in them (Matthew 25:1, 8). As the sun went down and evening became night, all ten of the women lit their lamps and waited. It took longer for the bridegroom to arrive than they had anticipated, so they all fell asleep. It wasn't until after midnight (which doesn't necessarily mean at 12:00 a.m.; in Greek it is μέσος *mesos* and can also mean in the middle of the night)[243] that the bridegroom finally arrived, and a cry went out, "Behold, the bridegroom cometh" (Matthew 25:6).

Because the bridegroom arrived so late, all of the lamps had burned out. The ten women woke up, anxious to join the caravan and head to the feast. They quickly trimmed their wicks and put more oil in their lamps. Well, five of them did. The other five didn't have any extra oil to put in their lamps. The five wise women had "oil in their vessels with their lamps" (Matthew 25:4). The five foolish asked the wise for some of their oil, but the wise answered, "Not so; lest there be not enough for us and you: but go ye rather to them that sell, and buy for yourselves" (Matthew 25:9). The foolish ran out into the night to find anyone who would sell them oil, and while they were gone, the bridegroom came. When they were finally able to make it to the marriage place, they knocked on the door and said, "Lord, Lord, open to us," and they were met with the response, "Verily I say unto you, I know you not" (Matthew 25:11–12). Now we have to take a minute to reflect on what we were just taught here. The foolish virgins weren't necessarily wicked. They just didn't realize how long the wait would be, and as a result, they didn't prepare properly. President Spencer W. Kimball explains this by pointing out that they were not "necessarily corrupt and reprobate, but they were knowing people who were foolishly unprepared for the vital happenings that were to affect their eternal lives. They had the saving, exalting gospel, but it had not been made the center of their lives. They knew the way but gave only a small measure of loyalty and devotion."[244] Those foolish virgins *have done virtuously* and were capable enough to have a lamp and some oil, just not enough oil for their vessel when it finally mattered.

This story used to make me sad, and I kind of thought the five wise virgins were rude for not sharing their oil. They could have at least walked together as a group to share the light. But President Kimball perfectly taught, "The kind of oil that is needed to illuminate the way and light up the darkness is not shareable. How can one share obedience to the principle of tithing; a mind at peace from righteous living; an accumulation of knowledge? How can one share faith or testimony? How can one share attitudes or chastity, or the experience of a mission? How can one share temple privileges? Each must obtain that kind of oil for himself [or herself]."[245]

All ten virgins had done virtuously, but the main difference between the two groups is that the wise endured to the end and the foolish did not. To endure means "to remain firm in a commitment to be true to the commandments of God despite temptation, opposition, and adversity."[246] The five wise women were not perfect, they just did their best to obtain oil. Drop by drop, experience by experience, these women endured to the end. And as a result, they *excellest them all.*

but thou excellest them all

The virtuous woman *excellest*, which means "to ascend, be exalted."[247] When we excel, we become exalted, and we get to live with our Heavenly Parents in the celestial kingdom. Speaking of how we get there, President Joseph Fielding Smith taught, "In order to obtain the exaltation we must accept the gospel and all its covenants; and take upon us the obligations which the Lord has offered; and walk in the light and the understanding of the truth; and 'live by every word that proceedeth forth from the mouth of God.'"[248] That is a virtuous woman. She has excelled, and now she will be welcomed in at the gates to sit down and have place with the Father and the Son. The realization of this incredible moment will often come after a lifetime of experiences, drops of oil, and endurance. But for a former student of mine, it came unexpectedly when she was only sixteen.

Madeline Hales was the ideal student. A darling sophomore at East High School in Salt Lake City, Utah, and in my seminary class. She was sweet, kind, popular, and friendly to everyone. She was a cheerleader, a member of the dance company, and an honor student. She had a mile-long smile and lit up every room she walked into. Her parents said, "Her primary focus in her life was obeying her Heavenly Father and following her Savior Jesus Christ. She loves the gospel and knows the joy that comes from serving others." That perfectly sums up Maddie. She was like the wise virgins; she had been carefully collecting her oil, and you could almost say that she had an overabundance of it. To all who knew her, she was ready and waiting to meet the Bridegroom; we just didn't think she would so soon.

In February of 2005, Maddie became extremely ill with flu-like symptoms. After about a week of not getting better, on Thursday, February 10, her mother took her to the hospital. Before she could make it through the doors, Maddie collapsed. She was diagnosed with bacterial meningitis. Word spread quickly, and many students were distressed. They held an outdoor vigil for her that night. An emergency fast was called. Many of the students caravanned to the temple to do baptisms for the dead. I've never seen anything quite like it. There was a run on temple recommends, and kids were going to the temple who had never gone before. Teenagers were petitioning the Lord, in His house, for the quick and miraculous recovery of Maddie. I can remember praying, "Please, Heavenly Father, please give them this miracle and build their foundation of faith. It would be so amazing and life changing!"

There was a stake-wide fast that Sunday, and I will never forget meeting together to break our fast. A crowd of teenagers and adults filled the chapel and gym, and when it was time to pray, like a wave, everyone fell to their knees, exercising their faith and pouring out their souls to God for a miracle. The next day, on the morning of February 14, 2005, Madeline Hales passed away, and so many hearts were broken. Is there a word that runs deeper than *devastation*? Because that is what everyone felt, including me.

Within an hour of Madeline's passing, her father called to let me know and to ask if I would be willing to speak at her funeral. Those six days before the funeral, I struggled to find words that would comfort the broken hearts of her friends and classmates who now questioned God, wondering where their miracle was. I fasted and prayed, asking God what I could possibly say that would matter or make a difference. Here is what God taught me: Maddie's example and her untimely death brought so many to Christ. I made a list of what I had witnessed leading up to her death:

- Teenagers who prayed.
- Teenagers who fasted, some for the first time. Many fasted for a full twenty-four hours.
- Teenagers who attended the temple, some for the first time.

- Teenagers who searched the scriptures for answers and comfort.
- Teenagers who formed new friendships, who felt an extraordinary sense of belonging, who pulled those on the fringes into their loving, faith-filled community.
- Teenagers who fulfilled their baptismal covenants as they mourned with those who mourned and comforted those who stood in need of comfort.

Is there anything more virtuous than these things? Reflecting back on that entire experience, none of us will deny the powerful impact of Maddie's death. It was an awe-inspiring experience to see how something so devastating could be filled with such light. For those of us who knew Maddie, we cannot doubt or wonder if her sixteen years were endurance enough to "excelleth them all." No doubt she will realize the words of Nephi, who says, "And if they endure unto the end they shall be lifted up at the last day, and shall be saved in the everlasting kingdom of the Lamb" (1 Nephi 13:37). Those students are now adults, and all of them were changed for the better because of this tragic event. Maddie's memory lives on, and those who knew her still visit her grave today.

I believe that as covenant-keeping women, all of us are doing virtuously during whatever time we are allotted in this life. We only have to do our own version of "the best," whatever that looks like. Verse 29 does not invite competition. It invites us to focus on obeying Heavenly Father and following our Savior, Jesus Christ. It invites us to love the gospel and know the joy that comes from serving others.

NOTES

30.

Favour is deceitful, and beauty is vain: but a woman that feareth the Lord, she shall be praised

30. שֶׁקֶר הַחֵן וְהֶבֶל הַיֹּפִי אִשָּׁה יִרְאַת־יְהוָה הִיא תִתְהַלָּל:

WHEN I TURNED EIGHT YEARS old, I received my very first journal. It was called the *All about Me* journal and was filled with writing prompts. One specific prompt asked, "If a fairy godmother suddenly appeared in my room one night and said I could have three wishes, I would wish . . ."

Well, I can assure you that it was not difficult for eight-year-old me to answer that question. Without hesitation, I wrote what my three wishes would be:

1. to be pretty

2. have nice close [clothes]

3. and be a better Mormon

Being pretty was my greatest desire, which clearly out-ranked my youthful religious zeal to "be a better mormon." Sadly, nothing has changed . . . for other little eight-year-old girls and at times, even for me.

Today there is so much value placed on beauty, but to meet its strict expectations seems impossible. When speaking to the women of the Church about beauty and size, Elder Jeffrey R. Holland said, "Frankly, the world has been brutal with you in this regard."[249] Brutal indeed! It is unfortunate that "beauty" has been defined for us without our consent, and many women struggle with trying to fit that definition. But what I love about verse 30 is that it contains the only obvious mention of the Lord in the proverb, and He is contrasted with *favour* and *beauty*.

Because we live in a world that rewards beauty and being well-liked, verse 30 could not come at a better time for us today. This verse offers us a new perspective on the role that *favour* and *beauty* should play in our lives. The last of the virtuous woman's attributes listed in the proverb is her ability to fear the Lord. This verse teaches us that fearing the Lord has everything to do with approaching the Savior and our relationship with Him, which is the most favorable and beautiful thing we can do.

Favour is deceitful, and beauty is vain

This verse begins with שֶׁקֶר (*sheqer*), which means "disappointment or falsehood."[250] This disappointment and falsehood are exactly what comes from *favour* or "the acceptance or finding favour in the eyes of man."[251] Sure, it feels good to be applauded, adored, praised, or liked, and social media has all the necessary trappings for the environment of favour to thrive. While serving as a member of the Seventy, Elder Gene R. Cook pointed out the "humblebrag," which is "an ostensibly modest or self-deprecating statement [or picture] whose actual purpose is to draw attention to something of which one is proud."252 Our world is filled with ways to find favour. But is it worth it?

President N. Eldon Tanner wrote, "How much more satisfying it is when we receive the praise of God, knowing that it is fully justified and that His love and respect for us will persist, when usually the praise of men is fleeting and most disappointing."253 Emphasizing the favour of man will always be fleeting and disappointing, and so will beauty, which is vain or *hebel:* "unsubstantial, worthless, and passing."254

The adversary carefully chooses his words as he whispers to each of us that we are not enough. He is no respecter of persons or age when it comes to those whom he seeks to make "miserable like unto himself" (2 Nephi 2:27).

However, those ugly feelings of insecurity and discouragement don't come from our Heavenly Father. To Him, we are beautiful. To Him, we are enough. Sister Elaine S. Dalton taught us about beauty when she said, "Deep beauty springs from virtue. . . . It is the kind of beauty that you see in the eyes of virtuous women. . . . It is a beauty that is earned through faith, repentance, and honoring covenants."255 It is the beauty that comes from being a converted and covenant-keeping woman filled with Christ's power. Fearing the Lord with a commitment to Him and His covenants is the most aesthetically pleasing thing we can do for ourselves.

but a woman that feareth the Lord

A woman who *feareth the Lord* stands in awe before, reverences, and honours Him.256 Godly fear, also known as "fear of the Lord" (Psalm 111:10; Isaiah 11:2–3) is equivalent to reverence and worship. The LDS Bible Dictionary teaches that this type of fear is "an essential part of the attitude of mind in which we ought to stand toward the All-holy God."[257] When we fear the Lord, we are blessed, for "the eye of the Lord is upon them that fear him" (Psalm 33:18). We are promised, "For thus saith the Lord—I, the Lord, am merciful and gracious unto those who fear me" (D&C 76:5). Elder David A. Bednar pointed out what this sublime reverence does for us: "Godly fear is a source of peace, assurance, and confidence."[258] We fear the Lord because we love the Lord. Two virtuous women in scripture that exemplified this *fear* are Shiphrah and Puah.

Shiphrah and Puah were Hebrew midwives who were commanded by the king of Egypt to kill all Hebrew baby boys at birth (Exodus 1:15–16). These two virtuous women refused to follow Pharaoh's command: "But the midwives *feared God*, and did not as the king of Egypt commanded them, but saved the men children alive" (Exodus 1:17; emphasis added), and by so doing, they put their own lives at risk. They cared not for the favour or praise of the king of Egypt; they only cared about the favour or praise of the all-holy God.

They were called in and asked by the king, "Why have ye done this thing, and have saved the men children alive?" (Exodus 1:18). Their response was quick and clever: "Because the Hebrew women are not as the Egyptian women; for they are lively, and are delivered ere the midwives come in unto them" (Exodus 1:19). Their reply "succeeded in deceiving Pharoah, saving the lives of countless Hebrew boys and protecting their own lives as a result."[259] The midwives' fear of God not only spared their lives but also blessed their houses. "Therefore God dealt well with the midwives: and the people multiplied, and waxed very mighty. And it came to pass, because the midwives feared God, that he made them houses" (Exodus 1:20–21). Making them houses indicates that they bore more than one child; these women were given children of their own. The midwives' reverence for the Lord gave them the peace, assurance, and confidence to do His will, and as a result, they *shall be praised*.

She shall be praised

Unlike the favor and praise of man, which won't last forever, the Lord's praise is real and enduring. Those who fear the Lord and seek to do His work *shall be praised*. This praise will be detailed in verse 31. Because the virtuous woman fears the Lord, He has taken notice of her, and she is highly valued by Him; His eye is upon her, He offers her much grace, many benefits are bestowed upon her, great honour is conferred upon her, and great goodness is laid up for her.[260]

When I was single and in college, I volunteered at a shelter for abused women and children. One of the women that I volunteered with was older and had raised all of her children. I would often ask her questions about raising kids and being married. One of her answers caught me off guard and taught me the only lesson I needed to know about these topics. She told me that the best thing I could do for my daughters is to raise them to become educated, confident, independent,

God-fearing women. At the time, three of the four made sense. After studying this verse and its meaning, and having four daughters of my own, I get it. Today, if a fairy godmother suddenly appeared in my room one night and said I could have three wishes, I would first wish for my daughters to be granted the beauty and favour that comes from fearing the Lord, the beauty and favour that comes from worshipping the all-holy God and caring only about what He thinks rather than what people on social media "like" or care about. I would then wish it for myself. And lastly, I would have to break the cardinal rule of wish-asking and ask for more wishes so I could wish it for everyone I know and come to know throughout the rest of my life.

NOTES

HER REWARD—
VERSE 31

31.

Give her of the fruit of her hands; and let her own works praise her in the gates.

31. תְּנוּ־לָהּ מִפְּרִי יָדֶיהָ וִיהַלְלוּהָ בַשְּׁעָרִים מַעֲשֶׂיהָ׃

VERSE 31 MAKES ME WANT to light two candles and say a prayer. One of the things that I love about the Jewish Sabbath rituals is the lighting of the Shabbat candles. Every Shabbat, it is tradition for women to light a minimum of two candles eighteen minutes before the sun goes down. They can also light a candle for every member of their family. If no woman is present, a man may perform the ritual. The two candles represent the words *remember*, זכור (*zakhor*), and *keep*, שמר (*shamor*), which come from the wording of the fourth commandment: "Remember the sabbath day, to keep it holy" (Exodus 20:8). After the candles are lit, the women draw their hands around the light of their candle and pull it toward their face three times. On the third time, they cover their eyes and pray. Then the men sing or recite "*Eshet Hayil*" (the proverb of a virtuous woman).

The light from a woman's candle represents Jehovah filling the room and surrounding her. She uses her hands to welcome Him in and then covers her eyes, acknowledging her fear and reverence before Jehovah. This ritual points to the bride, the virtuous woman, who is reverencing, remembering, and keeping her covenants in anticipation of the Bridegroom, Jesus Christ.

Verse 31 starts with the last letter in the Hebrew alphabet, ת (*tav*). This is the bookend of the proverb and explains the final result of all that the virtuous woman has done. This verse answers the question from verse 10, "Who can find a virtuous woman?" Now that her candles are lit, she awaits the Bridegroom and the moment when He will reward her for who she has become.

Give her of the fruit of her hands

This verse begins with the word *give* or תנו (*tenu*), which is a command form of the verb *to give*. "Give her what she deserves!" is right![261] Without hesitation, because of the fruit of her hands, the virtuous woman is to be given the "praise and glory that is due unto her."[262] The fruit of her hands is what Alma referred to as the "works of righteousness" (Alma 5:36). The fruit of her hands is the culmination of everything she has done as taught throughout the proverb. This is the final moment: her worth, herself and her household, her labors, her coverings, and her attributes will now stand as a witness of who she has become.

and let her own works praise her in the gates

This moment is her final judgment, and the gates (from way back in verse 23) are where this judgment takes place.

President Dallin H. Oaks explained, "The Final Judgment is not just an evaluation of the sum total of good and evil acts—what we have *done*. It is an acknowledgment of the final effect of our acts and thoughts—what we have *become*."263 The virtuous woman approaches the gates, where she sees Christ standing. Elder Jeffrey R. Holland described this moment this way: "True to the end, Christ lovingly claims those who have faith in him, and he advocates their cause before the great bar of justice."264 The virtuous woman's book of life is opened, and Jesus is at her side, standing as her advocate (see D&C 29:5). She comes unto God to "stand in the presence of him, to be judged of him according to the truth and holiness which is in him" (2 Nephi 2:10). Elder Dieter F. Uchtdorf described our judgment, saying, "I have confidence that we will not only be satisfied with the judgment of God; we will also be astonished and overwhelmed by His infinite grace, mercy, generosity, and love for us, His children. If our desires and works are good, if we have faith in a living God, then we can look forward to what Moroni called 'the pleasing bar of the great Jehovah, the Eternal Judge.'"265 This moment will be pleasing for everyone. God will give us our most desired outcome. He will allot unto us exactly what we *desire*, not necessarily what we "deserve."266

At that pleasing moment, a virtuous woman will be praised. But this is more than a "Hey, great job! You did it!" with God giving you a high five as you walk through the gates. This praise will cause us to shine.267 The Wisdom of Solomon says, "God tested them, and found them worthy of himself.

As gold in the furnace he proved them; . . . in the time of their visitation they shall shine forth."[268] On that day of judgment, we will be judged individually to determine our "shine," the eternal glory we will receive. Each degree of glory is compared to a certain degree of brightness: celestial = the sun, terrestrial = the moon, and telestial = the stars, but of the three degrees, the brightest one, the one that shines the most is the celestial. It is the shine that will come to those who are promised to "come forth in the morning of the First Resurrection."[269] A virtuous woman will inherit the celestial kingdom. She will be praised as she shines with the glory of the sun, and what a glorious day it will be!

The Lord taught Joseph Smith, "These are they who have come to an *innumerable company* of angels, to the general assembly and church of Enoch, and of the Firstborn" (D&C 76:67; emphasis added). The Apostle John saw "a *great multitude*, which no man could number, of all nations, and kindreds, and people, and tongues, stood before the throne, and before the Lamb, clothed with white robes, and palms in their hands; And cried with a loud voice, saying, Salvation to our God which sitteth upon the throne, and unto the Lamb" (Revelation 7:9–10; emphasis added). A virtuous woman will join the great multitude, the innumerable company of angels, the general assembly, and the church of the Firstborn. She will be among the righteous that "shall sit down in his kingdom, to go no more out; but their garments should be made white through the blood of the Lamb" (Alma 34:36). Covered in linen, purple, scarlet, and her priesthood power, she is ready to deliver her girdles to the Husband. Her tapestry and the fruit of her hands are proof that she loved the Husband with all her heart and she did Him good and not evil all the days of her life. She will now be invited into the gates, where she will be met with a loving and close embrace from Father. She will be invited to sit down and have an everlasting place with the Father and His Son. She will fulfill the promise given to Emma Smith in Doctrine and Covenants 25.[270]

In July 1830, Emma Smith received a revelation from the Lord through her husband, Joseph Smith. In that revelation, the Lord counseled Emma to "walk in the paths of virtue before me" (D&C 25:2). Walking in the path of virtue leads us to become *elect*, which is why the Lord called Emma "an elect lady" (D&C 25:3). *Elect* in this verse means "chosen," and this title is not reserved exclusively for her. The last verse of Doctrine and Covenants 25 says, "This is my voice unto all." So, every covenant-keeping daughter in God's kingdom is appropriately described as "an elect lady." Being an elect lady means that we have elected to follow the path of virtue laid out for us in this proverb, with our reward extending beyond any mortal comprehension.[271] Our promised blessings are the same as Emma's: "A crown of righteousness thou shalt receive" (D&C 25:15).

When my daughters were little, they were obsessed with princesses. I tried my hand at sewing a gown or two for them. But even with new dresses, in their minds, they weren't princesses until they had crowns. The crown was everything. Traditionally a Roman laurel crown was a symbol of victory and would be placed on the head of a victorious commander. An olive wreath crown was awarded to those who triumphed over their opponent in the Olympic games. These crowns imply that the wearer is great and mighty. How fitting, then, that several times in scripture, the Lord tells us that we will receive a crown of righteousness, eternal life, and glory (D&C 20:14; 29:13; 58:4). Our crown will be a symbol of our greatness, our victory. We truly triumphed over *the* opponent, and our crown will be a symbol of our "rightful place to rule, preside, or direct in the next life."[272]

On October 3, 1918, President Jospeh F. Smith was reading his scriptures and thinking about his son Hyrum Mack Smith, who had died earlier that year from a ruptured appendix at the age of forty-five.[273] As he sat pondering over the scriptures, he received a remarkable vision of the spirit world, now recorded as Doctrine and Covenants 138. In section 138, President Smith named many "great and mighty ones" who were assembled together in the spirit world. This verse in particular stands out to me: "And our glorious Mother Eve, with many of her faithful daughters who had lived through the ages and worshiped the true and living God" (D&C 138:39). To me, "glorious mother Eve" is the first example of a virtuous woman, and we, like many of those faithful daughters, follow her example. Eve brought her food from afar and was confident in her covenants, believing that she and her family would be strengthened to overcome any sorrow or disappointments they would face. She knew that the Savior's Atonement was the only way that families could be eternal. She knew by revelation the way back to our Heavenly Parents,[274] and today she stands with the vast congregation of the righteous (see D&C 138:39) awaiting that day of judgment to receive the fulness of joy. I imagine that we will all join with Eve as we fulfill the words of Isaiah and say, "I will greatly rejoice in the Lord, my soul shall be joyful in my God; for he hath clothed me in with the garments of salvation, he hath covered me with the robe of righteousness" (Isaiah 61:10).

So, light those candles and draw the Savior in.

This is what it means to be a virtuous woman.

This is why you are God's favorite!

NOTES

Endnotes

1 Russell M. Nelson, "Let God Prevail," *Ensign*, November 2020.

2 Carol A. Newsom, Sharon H. Ringe & Jacqueline E. Lapsley, *Women's Bible Commentary*, 3rd ed. (Louisville, KY: Westminster John Knox Press, 1991), 241.

3 Richard J. Clifford, *Proverbs: A Commentary* (Louisville, KY: Westminster John Knox Press, 1999); Roland Edmund Murphy, *World Biblical Commentary: Proverbs* (Nashville, TN: Thomas Nelson, 1998); Michael V. Fox, *The Anchor Yale Bible. A New Translation with Introduction and Commentary*, Proverbs 10–31, vol. 18B (New Haven, CT: Yale University Press, 2009), 1066; Katharine J. Dell, *The Book of Proverbs in Social and Theological Context* (Cambridge: University Press, 2006), 86–87. My allegorical interpretation of Proverbs 31 is not meant to question the original referentiality, rather I mean to look at its construction in terms of the "types" it utilizes. Using an "allegorical technique" when reading Proverbs 31 "does not avoid difficulties in the text . . . or to allow unbridled use of the human imagination. Rather, its use functions within a rule of faith (the *Theoria* in Greek terminology) as the language of faith seeks to penetrate the mystery of Christ's presence. The use of figuration (allegorical interpretation) "was assumed as a means by which the living Lord of scripture through the work of

the Holy Spirit continued to address each new generation through vigorous pursuit of the deeper significance of the words of scripture." See *The Bible as Christian Scripture: The Work of Brevard S. Childs,* ed. Christopher R. Seitz, and Harold, Richards Kent, Society of Biblical Literature, 2013. ProQuest eBook Central, http://ebookcentral.proquest.com/lib/asulib-ebooks/detail.action?docID=3118287. Created from asulib-ebooks on 2018–04–26 10:41:49.

4 *Women's Bible Commentary*, 3rd ed., 241.

5 Lowell L. Bennion, *The Unknown Testament* (Salt Lake City: Deseret Book, 1998), 97.

6 Ellis T. Rasmussen, *A Latter-Day Saint Commentary on the Old Testament* (Salt Lake City: Deseret Book, 1993), 484–485.

7 *World Biblical Commentary: Proverbs*, 249; *Proverbs: A Commentary*, 273.

8 "Christ as the bridegroom and the Church as his bride are dominant symbols throughout Old and New Testaments as well as modern scripture," S. Michael Wilcox, *Who Shall be Able to Stand?* (Salt Lake City: Deseret Book, 2003), 160; "The church must think of itself as a bride adorned for her husband . . . adorned as a bride for the Lamb of God as her husband" (Harold B. Lee, "Strengthen the Stakes of Zion," *Ensign*, July 1973); Marvin J. Ashton: "It can be properly and appropriately concluded that the ten virgins represent the people of the Church of Jesus Christ" ("A Time of Urgency," *Ensign*, May 1974); Spencer W. Kimball, *The Teachings of Spencer W. Kimball* (Salt Lake City: Deseret Book, 2002), 183.

9 Many commentators have noticed this literary device, for example, *World Biblical Commentary: Proverbs*, 245; R.N. Whybray, *The Composition of the Book of Proverbs* (Sheffield, England: Sheffield Academic Press, 1994), 153; *The Book of Proverbs in Social and Theological Context*, 85. For an example in the Old Testament that has retained the Hebrew letters in the King James translation, see Psalm 119.

10 See Roland E. Murphy, O. Carm, *The Tree of Life, An Exploration of Biblical Wisdom Literature* (Grand Rapids, MI: William B. Eerdmans Publishing, 2002), 26–27. Matthew Henry, *An Exposition of the Old and New Testament* (New York: R. Carter & Bros., 1853) vol. 3, 779, 781. *The Anchor Yale Bible. A New Translation with Introduction and Commentary*, Proverbs 10–31, vol. 18B, 275.

11 Matthew Henry, *An Exposition of the Old and New Testament* (New York: R. Carter & Bros., 1853) vol. 3, 779, 781. "Some think it was no part of the lesson which Lemuel's mother taught him, but a poem by itself, written by some other hand, and perhaps had been commonly repeated among the pious Jews, for the ease of which it was made alphabetical."

12 *The Tree of Life, An Exploration of Biblical Wisdom Literature*, 26–27. *The Anchor Bible. A New Translation with Introduction and Commentary*, Proverbs 10–31, vol. 18B, 2009, 275.

13 Each section/quintet is assigned a letter/number—Hebrew letters can also be numbers. א=1, ב=2, ג=3, etc.

14 Alonzo Gaskill, *The Lost Language of Symbolism: An Essential Guide for Recognizing and Interpreting Symbols of the Gospel* (Salt Lake City: Deseret Book, 2003), 120–121.

15 David Rolph Seely, *Doctrines of the Book of Mormon* (Salt Lake City: Deseret Book, 1992); "The Ten Commandments in the Book of Mormon," 1991 Sperry Symposium on the Book of Mormon, 167. See also Romans 13:8–10.

16 Ibid. "The 'tabernacle in the wilderness' profoundly reflects God's grace in its use of the number 5. This tabernacle, whose design was given directly by God, contained five curtains (Exodus 26:3), five bars (Exodus 26:26–27), five pillars and five sockets (Exodus 26:37), and an altar made of wood that was five cubits long and five cubits wide (Exodus 27:1). The height of the court within the tabernacle was five cubits (Exodus 27:18)," 167.

17 Francis Brown, S. R. Driver, and Charles A. Briggs, *The Brown-Driver-Briggs Hebrew and English Lexicon* (Peabody, MA: Hendrickson, 1997), 298. In the Greek text of the New Testament, the word for virtue is *dynamis*, which also means "power" or "strength." This word is used in Mark 5:30 when the Savior immediately knew someone had touched his clothes because "virtue had gone out of him." Christ's power or virtue was shared when he healed the woman with the issue of blood. Joseph Smith shared a similar experience. After giving blessings to the children of Jedediah M. Grant, the prophet turned pale and lost strength. Jedediah asked the prophet why he looked so spent. Joseph told him that in the process of giving the blessings he had seen "that Lucifer would exert his influence to destroy the children that I was blessing, and I strove with all the faith and spirit that I had to seal upon them a blessing that would secure their lives upon the earth; and so much virtue went out of me into the children, that I became weak, from which I have not yet recovered; and I referred to the case of the woman touching the hem of the garment of Jesus (Luke, 8th chapter). The virtue here referred to is the spirit of life; and a man, who exercises great faith in administering to the sick, blessing little children, or confirming, is liable to become weakened." *JS, History*, 1838–1856, vol. D-1 [1 August 1842–1 July 1843]. *History of the Church*, 5:303.

18 *The Anchor Bible. A New Translation with Introduction and Commentary*, Proverbs 10–31, vol. 18B, 891; *The Brown-Driver-Briggs Hebrew and English Lexicon*, 555.

19 *International Standard Bible Encyclopedia* (Grand Rapids, MI: W. B. Eerdmans, 1979), vol. II, "Dowry."

20 *The Brown-Driver-Briggs Hebrew and English Lexicon*, 819. See also Proverbs 3:15. The Septuagint translates this word as "precious gems," however, most commentators and early biblical scholars have interpreted this word as "pearl," connecting it to Matthew

7:6 and Matthew 13:45, see: *The Pulpit Commentary* (Grand Rapids, MI: Eerdmans, 1958); *Barnes' Notes on the Bible* (New York: Harper English, 1840); *John Gill's An Exposition of the Old Testament (1697–1771)* (Philadelphia, PA: William W. Woodward, 1978), 6 v., 28 cm., English. BYU Shaw-Shoemaker Microfiche Collection. The actual word for Ruby in Hebrew is perhaps דְּכֹד Kadkod: agate, ruby or precious stone as found in Isaiah 54:12 and Ezekiel 27:16, *The Brown-Driver-Briggs Hebrew and English Lexicon*, 461.

21 *Dictionary of Biblical Imagery* (Downers Grove, IL: InterVarsity Press, 1998), 633; *The Zondervan Pictorial Encyclopedia of the Bible* (Grand Rapids, MI: The Zondervan Corporation, 1975), vol. 4, M–P, "Pearl."

22 Jay A. Parry, Donald W. Parry, *Understanding the Book of Revelation* (Salt Lake City: Deseret Book, 2007), 296.

23 Michael V. Fox, *The Anchor Yale Bible. A New Translation with Introduction and Commentary,* Proverbs 10–31, vol. 18B, 892.

24 *Old Testament Seminary Teacher Manual* (1998) Proverbs 1–31, 160–161.

25 *The Brown-Driver-Briggs Hebrew and English Lexicon*, 127.

26 Richard K. Hart, "The Marriage Metaphor," *Ensign*, January 1995.

27 Jeffrey R. Holland, *Christ and the New Covenant: The Messianic Message of the Book of Mormon* (Salt Lake City: Deseret Book, 1997), 290.

28 *Old Testament Student Manual Kings–Malachi*, (1982), 103–110. See Notes and Commentary on Hosea 10–2.

29 Frank Moore Cross, *From Epic to Canon, History and Literature in Ancient Israel* (Baltimore, MD: The Johns Hopkins University Press, 1998), 13.

30 Ibid., 13–14.

31 "The Power of Covenants," *Ensign*, May 2009.

32 See also Doctrine and Covenants 18:42, 20:71, 68:25.

33 D. Todd Christofferson, "The Power of Covenants," *Ensign*, May 2009.

34 Joy D. Jones, "An Especially Noble Calling," *Ensign*, May 2020.

35 Russell M. Nelson, "Let God Prevail," *Ensign*, November 2020.

36 Barbara Morgan Gardner, *The Priesthood Power of Women: In the Temple, Church, and Family* (Salt Lake City: Deseret Book, 2019), 88.

37 Exodus 12:36; Numbers 31:9; Deuteronomy 2:35, 13:16, 20:14; 1 Samuel 14:32, 17:53; 2 Samuel 3:22; 2 Kings 7:16; *The Brown-Driver-Briggs Hebrew and English Lexicon*, "spoil" or "booty," 1021; "need," "lack," 341; or "possibly gain."

38 Russell M. Nelson, "Spiritual Treasures," *Ensign*, November 2019.

39 *The Anchor Bible. A New Translation with Introduction and Commentary*, Proverbs 10–31, vol. 18B, 893; *Proverbs: A Commentary*, 275.

40 *The Brown-Driver-Briggs Hebrew and English Lexicon*, 168.

41 Jeff A. Benner, *Faith*, Ancient Hebrew Research Center, ancient-hebrew.org.

42 This concept of answering in the Savior's name "I Am" was originally introduced to me as a student of Dr. Susan Easton Black in her Doctrine and Covenants REL. C 324, October 1994.

43 *The Brown-Driver-Briggs Hebrew and English Lexicon*, 225.

44 Larry R. Lawrence, "What Lack I Yet?" *Ensign*, November 2015.

45 *The Brown-Driver-Briggs Hebrew and English Lexicon*, 948.

46 *John Gill's Exposition of the Old Testament* (1697–1771), (Philadelphia: William W. Woodward), 1978, 6 v.; 28 cm., English. BYU Shaw-Shoemaker Microfiche Collection.

47 *The Brown-Driver-Briggs Hebrew and English Lexicon*, 398–399.

48 Elaine L. Jack, "Ponder the Path of Thy Feet," *Ensign*, November 1993.

49 *The Brown-Driver-Briggs Hebrew and English Lexicon*, 205. When a Hebrew root word is followed by the suffix ה it ascribes it to being

a feminine noun or action. For example: שרדה means "she seeks." This is seen throughout the proverb.

50 Donald W. Parry, Jay A. Parry, Tina M Peterson, *Understanding Isaiah* (Salt Lake City: Deseret Book, 1998), 18–19.

51 The curtains (Exodus 26:1), veil (Exodus 26:31), and outer door hangings (Exodus 26:36) of the tabernacle were all made of linen. Similarly, the priest's holy temple clothing (i.e., the ephod, coats, mitre, bonnets, and breeches) were made of fine linen (Exodus 28:42, 39:2, 27–28). These items were called the "holy garments" (Leviticus 16:4, 32). Also in the book of Revelation the "seven angels" that came forth from the heavenly temple, the armies of heaven, and the Saints of God all are "arrayed in fine linen, clean and white" (Revelation 15:6, 19:7–8, 14). The crucified body of Jesus was wrapped and buried in linen cloth (Matthew 27:59–60).

52 Joseph Fielding McConkie, Donald W. Parry, *A Guide to Scriptural Symbols*, (Salt Lake City: Bookcraft, 1990), 79.

53 Richard D. Draper, "Witness of Jesus Christ," *Sperry Symposium on the Old Testament*, 1989); Edward J. Brandt, Correlation Department of The Church of Jesus Christ of Latter-day Saints "The Law of Moses and the Law of Christ," 24.

54 *The Lost Language of Symbolism, Clothing as Symbols*, Chapter 4 note 10.

55 Joseph Anderson, "Strength of the Spirit," *Ensign*, May 1974.

56 *The Brown-Driver-Briggs Hebrew and English Lexicon*, 343.

57 Ibid., 496.

58 First Presidency Letter "Ministering with Strengthened Melchizedek and Priesthood Quorums and Relief Societies," April 2, 2018.

59 Jean B. Bingham, "Ministering as the Savior Does," *Ensign*, May 2018.

60 Russell M. Nelson, "A Plea to My Sisters," *Ensign*, November 2015.

61 Gordon B. Hinckley, "Stay the Course—Keep the Faith," *Ensign*, November 1995.

62 Gordon B. Hinckley, "Feed the Spirit, Nourish the Soul," *Ensign*, October 1998.

63 Bible Dictionary, "Shipping," 774.

64 *The Brown-Driver-Briggs Hebrew and English Lexicon*, 536. *The Anchor Yale Bible. A New Translation with Introduction and Commentary*, Proverbs 10–31, vol. 18B, 894.

65 *The Brown-Driver-Briggs Hebrew and English Lexicon*, 598, 935.

66 Jeffrey R. Holland, "To Young Women," *Ensign*, November 2005.

67 In Hebrew, this verse begins with the letter *vav* וֹ. When a *vav* is prefixed directly to a word, it is translated as "and" or "then." When the *vav* in this verse is attached to a perfect verb, it makes verses 14 and 15 a narrative sequence. It can also indicate a change in verb tense implying that her actions are ongoing.

68 *World Biblical Commentary: Proverbs*, 247.

69 *The Anchor Yale Bible. A New Translation with Introduction and Commentary*, Proverbs 10–31, vol. 18B, 275.

70 *The Brown-Driver-Briggs Hebrew and English Lexicon*, 877–878. The verb for "to rise" is *Qum*; the form in this verse is a future, active tense.

71 This word can also be pronounced layeleh. *The Brown-Driver-Briggs Hebrew and English Lexicon*, 538. See also Micah 3:6; Job 35:10; 36:20; Isaiah 21:11–12.

72 *The Brown-Driver-Briggs Hebrew and English Lexicon*, 382.

73 *The Lost Language of Symbolism*, 3. *Guide to Scriptural Symbols*, "meat." Meat also means the mysteries of the gospel. It is for those who have a mature knowledge of the doctrines of the gospel and are able to digest "the greater portion of the word" of God (Alma 12:10).

74 Addie Fuhriman, "Singleness: How Relief Society Can Help," *Ensign*, November 1980.

75 *The Brown-Driver-Briggs Hebrew and English Lexicon*, 655.

76 Siddur, "Morning Blessings," 7.

77 Ross Baron, Education Week, August 3, 2018. https://video.byui.edu/media/Ross+Baron+-+Education+Week+2018+-+Friday+Address/0_rb664x7u/32573922.

78 Harold B. Lee, "A Blessing for the Saints," *Ensign*, January 1973.

79 *World Biblical Commentary: Proverbs*, 247.

80 *The Brown-Driver-Briggs Hebrew and English Lexicon*, 273.

81 *Proverbs: A Commentary*, 275.

82 Further referenced, "Concerning the parable of the wheat and of the tares . . . the field was the world" (Doctrine and Covenants 86:1–2). Similarly, Lehi beheld in a dream, "a large and spacious field, as if it had been a world" (1 Nephi 8:20).

83 *A Guide to Scriptural Symbols*, "Field."

84 *The Brown-Driver-Briggs Hebrew and English Lexicon*, 542–543.

85 Ibid., 826.

86 Ibid., 642

87 Guide to the Scriptures, "Vineyard," https://www.churchofjesuschrist.org/scriptures/gs/vineyard-of-the-lord?lang=eng. See also, Isaiah 5:7; Matthew 20:1–16; Jacob 5; Jacob 6; Doctrine and Covenants 21:9.

88 Thomas S. Monson, "Welcome to Conference," *Ensign*, November 2013.

89 Joanne B. Doxey, "Strengthening the Family," *Ensign*, November 1987.

90 Russell M. Nelson, "An Outpouring of the Spirit," *Ensign*, March 2017.

91 Robin Scott Jensen, "A Bit of String," https://history.churchofjesuschrist.org/content/museum/a-bit-of-old-string?lang=eng.

92 *The Anchor Yale Bible*. A *New Translation with Introduction and Commentary*, Proverbs 10–31, vol. 18B, 894.

93 Philip Babcock Grove, *Webster's Third New International Dictionary of the English Language Unabridged* (Springfield, MA: Merriam-Webster Inc., 2002).

94 See D. Todd Christofferson, "The Power of Covenants," *Ensign*, May 2009.

95 *The Brown-Driver-Briggs Hebrew and English Lexicon*, 55.

96 Ibid., 284.

97 Gene R. Cook, "The Grace of the Lord," *The New Era*, December 1988.

98 Girding up ones loins is traditionally masculine, and the term also makes reference to girding one's loins for warfare. "They shall fight manfully" supports this idea, but since all scripture is for profit and learning and is applicable to all (1 Nephi 19:23), girding up ones loins can also be feminine. See "Likening the Scriptures to our Personal Lives," *Ensign*, March 2009.

99 D. Todd Christofferson, "The Power of Covenants," *Ensign*, May 2009.

100 James Goldberg, *The Autobiography of Jane Manning James, Seven Decades of Faith and Devotion*. Dec. 11, 2013. https://history.churchofjesuschrist.org/article/jane-manning-james-life-sketch?lang=eng.

101 Kenneth W. Godfrey, Audrey M. Godfrey, Jill Mulvay Derr, *Women's Voices: An Untold History of the Latter-day Saints 1830–1900* (Salt Lake City: Deseret Book, 1982), *Patience Loader (Roza Archer)* 241–242.

102 Erica Palmer, "Descendants of Mormon Pioneer John Rowe Moyle 'Learn they can do hard things,'" *Deseret News*, August 7, 2014.

103 In Gene A. Sessions, ed., "Biographies and Reminiscences from the James Henry Moyle Collection," typescript, Church Archives, The Church of Jesus Christ of Latter-day Saints, 203 & Frank Essom, *Pioneers and Prominent Men of Utah*, 1913, 1049.

104 *World Biblical Commentary: Proverbs*, 247.

105 See Dieter F. Uchtdorf. "The Power of a Personal Testimony," *Ensign*, November 2006.

106 *The Brown-Driver-Briggs Hebrew and English Lexicon*, 380.

107 Edgar Swift and Angela M. Kinney, eds. *The Vulgate Bible Volume III, The Poetical Books: Douay-Rheims Translation*, Proverbs 31, Dumbarton Oaks Medieval Library, 2011.

108 Rev. Joseph Benson, *Benson's Commentary on the Old and New Testaments* vol. 1: Genesis 1:25, 31 (New York: G. Lane & C.B. Tippett, 1846), 20.

109 Helvecio Martins, "The Value of a Testimony," *Ensign*, November 1990.

110 Joseph B. Wirthlin, *Finding Peace in our Lives* (Salt Lake City: Deseret Book, 1995), 77.

111 See Boyd K. Packer, "Candle of the Lord," *Mission Presidents Seminar*, 1982.

112 *The Anchor Yale Bible. A New Translation with Introduction and Commentary*, Proverbs 10–31, vol. 18B, 895.

113 *The Brown-Driver-Briggs Hebrew and English Lexicon*, 538.

114 See Karen Lynn Davidson, *Our Latter-Day Hymns: The Stories and the Messages* (Salt Lake City: Bookcraft, 1988), 322–323; and The Tabernacle Choir, *Keep the Lower Lights Burning*, March 16, 2014, http://home.uchicago.edu/~coleman/public_html/lowerlights.html.

115 Jane Mcbride Choate, "Heroes and Heroines," *Liahona,* September 1987; Jaynann Morgan Payne, "Eliza R. Snow, First Lady of the Pioneers," *Ensign*, September 1973.

116 This quotation is popularly attributed to Joseph F. Smith, but the specific source is unknown. Smith spoke of Elmina S. Taylor in similar terms at her funeral: "Most people of my acquaintance . . . walk very largely in a light that is borrowed. . . . She was one of the few in the world who had the light within her . . . and she walked in it" ("Death of Elmina S. Taylor," *Improvement Era* 8, no. 3 [January 1905]): 221; see also Joseph F. Smith, *Gospel Doctrine: Selections from the Sermons and Writings of Joseph F. Smith* (Salt Lake City: Deseret Book, 1978), 87–88.

117 "The Lord Is My Trust," *Poems, Religious, Historical, and Political*, vol. 1 (1856), 148–149; italicized emphasis in original.

118 *The Anchor Yale Bible. A New Translation with Introduction and Commentary*, Proverbs 10–31, vol. 18B, 895.

119 *Proverbs: A Commentary*, 275.

120 *The Brown-Driver-Briggs Hebrew and English Lexicon*, 388–389.

121 *The Septuagint Version Old Testament and Apocrypha with an English Translation; and Various Readings and Critical Notes*; (Grand Rapids, MI: Zondervan Publishing House, 1976), 818.

122 J. J. Stewart Perowne, *The Cambridge Bible for schools and colleges* (Cambridge, MA: University Press, 1889), BYU HBL Library, Special Archives. In the Hebrew translation, the word *distaff* comes before *spindle*, but it is specific to there being a spindle and distaff, both being a familiar part of everyday life in biblical times. Of the two Hebrew words used here, the first occurs nowhere else, but it is derived from a root which means to be straight and therefore may properly denote the distaff, or straight rod. Of the second word, the root-meaning is to be round. It is used of the circuit or circle round, the environs of, Jerusalem (Nehemiah 3:12, 17).

123 *World Biblical Commentary: Proverbs*, 247; "The word for *distaff* and *spindle* are hapax."

124 David A. Bednar, "That We May Always Have His Spirit to Be with Us," *Ensign*, May 2006.

125 Book of Commandments, 1833. JSP, R2:3–172 "Book of Commandments, 1833," 19, *The Joseph Smith Papers*, http://www.josephsmithpapers.org/paper-summary/book-of-command-ments-1833/23.

126 See Robert C. Fuller, *Spiritual, but Not Religious: Understanding Unchurched America* (New York: Oxford University Press, 2001), 15, 17; see also, Mark Ashurst-McGee, "A Pathway to Prophethood: Joseph Smith Junior as Rodsman, Village Seer,

and Judeo-Christian Prophet" (master's dissertation, Utah State University, 2000), 126–148.

127 Usually called the *Rod of Aaron*, this rod was carried by Aaron and was sometimes called the rod of God (Exodus 4:20; 7:10, 12, 19; 8:5, 16; 17:9; Numbers 17:6–10).

128 *Teachings of Presidents of the Church: Joseph Smith* [2007], 132.

129 David A. Bednar, "The Spirit of Revelation," *Ensign*, May 2011.

130 Ronald A. Rasband, "Let the Holy Spirit Guide," *Ensign*, May 2017.

131 *Joseph Smith Papers*, Nauvoo Relief Society Minute Book, Page 6, 17 March 1842. https://www.josephsmithpapers.org/paper-summary/nauvoo-relief-society-minute-book/3#XE364A107–8BCD-4116-BFFA-E9126CD21AF2.

132 Sheri Dew & Virginia H. Pearce, *The Beginning of Better Days: Divine Instruction to Women from the Prophet Joseph Smith* (Salt Lake City: Deseret Book, 2012), 93.

133 *Joseph Smith Papers*, Nauvoo Relief Society Minute Book, https://www.josephsmithpapers.org/paper-summary/nauvoo-relief-society-minute-book/9.

134 Ibid., 63, http://www.josephsmithpapers.org/paper-summary/nauvoo-relief-society-minute-book/60.

135 *The Brown-Driver-Briggs Hebrew and English Lexicon*, 776.

136 Ibid., 2.

137 Jeffrey R. Holland, "Broken Things to Mend," *Ensign*, May 2006.

138 Henry B. Eyring, "Come unto Christ," *Ensign*, March 2008.

139 James E. Talmage, *Jesus the Christ* (Salt Lake City: Deseret Book, 1982), 242.

140 The exact author of this quote is unknown, although some think Mae West allegedly said it.

141 David A. Bednar, "Bear Up Their Burdens with Ease," *Ensign*, May 2014.

142 Neal A. Maxwell, "Endure It Well," *Ensign*, May 1990.

143 Susette Fletcher Green, Dawn Hall Anderson, Patricia T. Holland, *To Rejoice as Women* (Talks from the 1994 BYU Women's Conference), 99–100().

144 *The Brown-Driver-Briggs Hebrew and English Lexicon*, 1017. *The Lost Language of Symbolism: An Essential Guide for Recognizing and Interpreting Symbols of the Gospel, Colors as Symbols*, Notes to Chapter 5, note 110, 355. Most Hebrew words for color originate from the world around them. "The ancient Hebrews experienced color primarily through nature; colors suggested to them elements of the physical world. Blue was the color of the sky, green the color of grass and plants, red the color of blood, white the color of wool and snow."

145 Job 38:22–23, *Dictionary of Biblical Imagery* (Downers Grove, IL: InterVarsity Press, 1998), 2696–2698; "What Does Snow Symbolize?" Reference, https://www.reference.com/world-view/snow-symbolize-23c1598d88e76e13.

146 *A Guide to Scriptural Symbols*, 33; Joseph Fielding McConkie, *Gospel Symbolism* (Salt Lake City: Deseret Book, 1999), 256–257.

147 *The Anchor Yale Bible. A New Translation with Introduction and Commentary*, Proverbs 10–31, vol. 18B, 896.

148 *The Lost Language of Symbolism: An Essential Guide for Recognizing and Interpreting Symbols of the Gospel*, 90–92.

149 *Teachings of Joseph F. Smith*, Ch. 11 "Jesus Christ Redeems the Repentant from Spiritual Death," 98.

150 Neal A. Maxwell, *Meek and Lowly* (Salt Lake City: Deseret Book, 1987), 11.

151 Permission granted by Tami Weaver for the retelling of this story.

152 *The Brown-Driver-Briggs Hebrew and English Lexicon*, 915. Proverbs 31:22, 7:16.

153 *John Gill's An Exposition of the Old Testament* (1697–1771), (Philadelphia: William W. Woodward, 1978), 6 v.; 28 cm., English. BYU Shaw-Shoemaker Microfiche Collection.

154 Robert D. Hales, "Becoming a Disciple of Our Lord Jesus Christ," *Ensign*, May 2017.

155 *The Brown-Driver-Briggs Hebrew and English Lexicon*, 1058.

156 Jay A. Parry, Donald W. Parry, *Understanding the Signs of the Times* (Salt Lake City: Deseret Book, 1999), 73.

157 Hugh Nibley, *Approaching Zion* (Salt Lake City: Deseret Book, 1989), 559. This practice still exists among Bedouin and nomadic tribes.

158 Ibid. The significance of this custom adds to the story of the woman, Jael, found in Judges 4:18–21. Sisera, the enemy and Captain of the Host, felt safe in Jael's tent due to a treaty of peace, but the Hebrew makes the story much more significant. Sisera ran into the tent of Jael seeking refuge and a place to hide. As a ruse she welcomed him in and "covered him with a mantle." She offered him protection which is why he felt safe enough to accept a drink of milk and take a nap. "Safe enough" to not have any fears—but the act was a ruse, for in his sleep he had a nail hammered into his temples (Judges 4:21). Jael's action ended the war and freed the Israelites.

159 Frank Moore Cross, *From Epic to Canon: History and Literature in Ancient Israel*, 12–13; see *Biblical Archaeology Review*, July/August 1999, vol. 25, Issue 4. Jehovah or God as the Divine Kinsman and our tribal affiliation with Him was first explored by religious scholar Frank Moore Cross.

160 *Approaching Zion*, 558–559. Most interesting is the Arabic *kafata*, as it is the key to a dramatic situation.

161 *World Biblical Commentary: Proverbs*, 247. *The Anchor Yale Bible. A New Translation with Introduction and Commentary*, Proverbs 10–31, vol. 18B, 896.

162 Cecil Frances Alexander, John H. Gower, 1855–1922, "There is a Green Hill Far Away," (*Hymns*, no. 194).

163 *The Brown-Driver-Briggs Hebrew and English Lexicon*, 393. The verb form used here is *Niphal*.

164 *Proverbs: A Commentary*, 276.

165 *John Gill's An Exposition of the Old Testament* (1697–1771), (Philadelphia: William W. Woodward, 1978), 6 v.; 28 cm., English. BYU Shaw-Shoemaker Microfiche Collection; italics added.

166 Ibid.

167 Cooper, *An Illustrated Encyclopedia of Traditional Symbols*, 73; See also *Door of the Sheep*; part 1: Gate.

168 *Jesus the Christ*, 597–598.

169 Dennis A Wright, "The Prophet's Voice of Authority" in The 26th Annual Sydney B. Sperry Symposium, *Voices of Old Testament Prophets* (Salt Lake City: Deseret Book Company, 1997), 43–44.

170 Andrew C. Skinner, *Prophets, Priests and Kings: Old Testament Figures Who Symbolize Christ* (Salt Lake City: Deseret Book Company, 2006); Chapter 5: *Abraham, Isaac and Jacob—Fathers of the Faithful*, 44.

171 *The Brown-Driver-Briggs Hebrew and English Lexicon*, 497.

172 Hugh W. Nibley and John W. Welch, *Teachings of the Book of Mormon, Semesters 1–4, with 5 lectures by John W. Welch* (lectures 97–101). *Lectures presented to an Honors Book of Mormon class at Brigham Young University, 1988–1990* (Provo, UT: Foundation for Ancient Research & Mormon Studies, 1993), 271–272.

173 David Noel Freedman, *The Anchor Bible Dictionary*. vol. 2, Clothing (New York: Doubleday, 1992); Joseph and Aseneth 3:9. The Bible also mentions the special garments worn by the bride for her wedding (see Isaiah 49:18; 61:10; Jeremiah 2:32; Revelation 21:2, Doctrine and Covenants 109:74).

174 *The Brown-Driver-Briggs Hebrew and English Lexicon*, 690.

175 *The Anchor Yale Bible. A New Translation with Introduction and Commentary*, Proverbs 10–31, vol. 18B, 896.

176 H. F. D. Sparks (ed.), *The Apocryphal Old Testament* (Oxford: Oxford University Press, 1984), 473–503; David Cooke, Dr. Mark Goodacre, *Joseph and Aseneth*: II, III, V, 465–503.

177 Donald W. Parry, *Temples of the Ancient World: Ritual and Symbolism* (Salt Lake City: Deseret Book, 1994), 676–677; David Cooke, Dr. Mark Goodacre *Joseph and Aseneth* III.

178 *The Brown-Driver-Briggs Hebrew and English Lexicon*, 569.

179 *The Brown-Driver-Briggs Hebrew and English Lexicon*, 292. It is important to note that in the Hebrew text of this verse the word is actually singular; it does not have a plural ending. Plurals and singulars in Hebrew are fluid.

180 Donald W. Parry, *Temples of the Ancient World: Ritual and Symbolism* (Salt Lake City: Deseret Book, 1994), Stephen D. Ricks, "The Garment of Adam in Jewish, Muslim, and Christian Tradition," 713–714.

181 *The Apocryphal Old Testament*, 473–503, *Joseph and Aseneth* XIV.

182 Ibid.

183 *Joseph and Aseneth* 14:15, Walter A. Elwell, *Evangelical Dictionary of Theology* (Grand Rapids, MI: Baker Academic, 2001), 742. *From Epic to Canon, History and Literature in Ancient Israel*, 13.

184 *The Brown-Driver-Briggs Hebrew and English Lexicon*, 688.

185 Bible Dictionary, "Peculiar," 748. President Russell M. Nelson shared, "For us to be identified by servants of the Lord as his *peculiar* people is a compliment of the highest order." Russell M. Nelson, "Children of the Covenant," *Ensign*, May 1995.

186 Jeffrey R. Holland, "The Other Prodigal," *Ensign*, May 2002.

187 "How to Help Young Women Feel Valued and Needed in the Church," September 22, 2017, https://www.youtube.com/watch?v=TVM8Cke05OU&t=204s.

188 Ibid.

189 *The Brown-Driver-Briggs Hebrew and English Lexicon*, 738.

190 Ibid., 214.

191 Russell M. Nelson, "Spiritual Treasures," *Ensign*, November 2019.

192 *The Priesthood Power of Women: In the Temple, Church, and Family*, 94.

193 Hugh Nibley, *Patriarchy and Matriarchy, Old Testament and Related Studies* (Salt Lake City: Deseret Book, 1986), 88.

194 Ibid., 93.

195 R. David Freedman, "Woman, a Power Equal to Man," *Biblical Archeology Review* 9:1, Jan./Feb. 1983, 56–58.

196 Jean B. Bingham, "United in Accomplishing God's Work," *Ensign* or *Liahona*, May 2020.

197 Ibid.

198 BYU Studies vol. 14 (1973–1974) in a presentation by Buddy Youngreen. According to his source he got it from: Bailey, *Emma Hale*, 112–113. (A copy of the blessing is also on file in the Historical Department of the Church, Salt Lake City, UT.)

199 Ibid.

200 *The Brown-Driver-Briggs Hebrew and English Lexicon*, 30.

201 H. D. M. Spence-Jones, Joseph S. Exell, and Edward Mark Deems, *The Pulpit Commentary* (Grand Rapids, MI: Eerdmans, 1958), 601.

202 *The Priesthood Power of Women: In the Temple, Church, and Family*, 118, 16.

203 Russell M. Nelson, "Let God Prevail," *Liahona*, November 2020.

204 See Jean B. Bingham, "United in Accomplishing God's Work," *Ensign*, May 2020.

205 *The Brown-Driver-Briggs Hebrew and English Lexicon*, 804.

206 Russell M. Nelson, "A Plea to My Sisters," *Ensign*, November 2015.

207 *Contributor*, vol. 13 (November 1891–October 1892) vol. XIII. June 1892, No. 8, Deseret Book Company 2021.

208 *The Brown-Driver-Briggs Hebrew and English Lexicon*, 435.

209 *World Biblical Commentary: Proverbs*, 248.

210 Ibid., 338.

211 D. Kelly Ogden, Jared W. Ludlow, Kerry Muhlestein, eds., *The Gospel of Jesus Christ in the Old Testament* (Salt Lake City: Deseret Book, 2009). Daniel L. Belnap, "How Excellent Is Thy

Lovingkindness": *The Gospel Principle of Hesed*, Sydney B. Sperry Symposium.

212 D. Kelly Ogden, Jared W. Ludlow, Kerry Muhlestein, eds., *The Gospel of Jesus Christ in the Old Testament* (Salt Lake City: Deseret Book, 2009). Daniel L. Belnap, "How Excellent Is Thy Lovingkindness": *The Gospel Principle of Hesed*, Sydney B. Sperry Symposium. See also Susan Schept, "Hesed: Feminist Ethics in Jewish Tradition," in *Conservative Judaism* 57 (2004), 21–29.

213 Some believe that this was a sexual euphemism, but when Boaz ivites her to stay until morning, the writer does not use the word for lying down (see Ruth 3:13) but rather for lodging—a word that never carries sexual connotations in the Hebrew Bible. See Kerry Muhlestein, "Ruth, Redemption, Covenant, and Christ," Sydney B. Sperry Symposium.

214 Kerry Muhlestein, "Ruth, Redemption, Covenant, and Christ," Sydney B. Sperry Symposium.

215 *Sunday on Monday*, Season 1 Episode 10.

216 M. Russell Ballard, "Women of Dedication, Faith, Determination, and Action," BYU Women's Conference Address, May 2015.

217 See D. Todd Christofferson, CES devotional address, "Saving Your Life," Brigham Young University, September 14, 2014.

218 Russell M. Nelson, "A Plea to My Sisters," *Ensign*, November 2015.

219 *The Brown-Driver-Briggs Hebrew and English Lexicon*, 859.

220 Ibid., 237.

221 *Old Testament Student Manual; Kings—Malachi*, "Chapter 26 Ezekiel: Watchman of Israel," 265.

222 J. J. Stewart Perowne, *The Cambridge Bible for Schools and Colleges* (Cambridge: University Press, 1889), BYU HBL Library, Special Archives.

223 Joseph Benton, G. Lane & C.B. Tippett, Benson, *Commentary on the Old and New Testaments* (New York: T. Carlton & J. Porter, 1867), Proverbs 31:28, 1155.

224 Dieter F. Uchtdorf, "Of Things That Matter Most," *Ensign*, November 2010.

225 Ronald A. Rasband, "Build a Fortress of Spirituality and Protection," *Ensign*, May 2019.

226 *World Biblical Commentary: Proverbs*, 248.

227 *The Brown-Driver-Briggs Hebrew and English Lexicon*, 119–122.

228 Sheri L. Dew "Are We Not All Mothers?" *Ensign*, November 2001.

229 Lesson 52: 1 John, 2 John, 3 John, and Jude," *New Testament Teacher Manual* (2014).

230 *The Brown-Driver-Briggs Hebrew and English Lexicon*, 877.

231 "Ashar," *The Brown-Driver-Briggs Hebrew and English Lexicon*, 80.

232 Von G. Keetch, "Blessed and Happy Are Those Who Keep the Commandments of God," *Ensign*, November 2015.

233 "History, 1838–1856, volume D-1 [1 August 1842–1 July 1843] [addenda]," 3 [addenda], *The Joseph Smith Papers*, accessed November 28, 2018, https://www.josephsmithpapers.org/paper-summary/history-1838–1856-volume-d-1–1-august-1842–1-july-1843/284.

234 JoAnn Jolley, "Women Meet at BYU 'For Such a Time As This.'" BYU Women's Conference, April 1982.

235 C.S. Lewis, *Mere Christianity* (New York: Touchstone, 1996), 175–176.

236 Richard G. Scott, "The Atonement Can Secure Your Peace and Happiness," *Ensign*, November 2006.

237 Sheri Dew, *Insights from a Prophet's Life: Russell M. Nelson* (Salt Lake City: Deseret Book, 2019), 227.

238 Russell M. Nelson, "Joy and Spiritual Survival," *Ensign*, November 2016.

239 *The Brown-Driver-Briggs Hebrew and English Lexicon*, 237.

240 See Donald W. Parry, *Preserved in Translation: Hebrew and Other Ancient Literary Forms in the Book of Mormon* (Religious Studies Center, Brigham Young University: Deseret Book, 2020), 7.

241 Quoted in Quentin L. Cook. "Personal Peace: The Reward of Righteousness," *Ensign*, May 2013.

242 *The Brown-Driver-Briggs Hebrew and English Lexicon*, 913.

243 "μέσος," James Strong, *Strong's Exhaustive Concordance of the Bible* (Peabody, MA: Hendrickson Publishers, 2009), *G3319*, 1647.

244 Spencer W. Kimball, *Faith Precedes the Miracle* (Salt Lake City: Deseret Book, 1972), 254.

245 Ibid., 255–256.

246 Guide to the Scriptures, "Endure," scriptures.churchofjesuschrist.org.

247 *The Brown-Driver-Briggs Hebrew and English Lexicon*, 748.

248 Joseph Fielding Smith, ed. Bruce R. McConkie, *Doctrines of Salvation* (Salt Lake City: Deseret Book, 1955), 2:43.

249 Jeffrey R. Holland, "To Young Women," *Ensign*, November 2005.

250 *The Brown-Driver-Briggs Hebrew and English Lexicon*, 1055.

251 Ibid., 336.

252 Gene R. Cook, "The Eternal Everyday," *Ensign*, November 2017.

253 N. Eldon Tanner, "For They Loved the Praise of Men More Than the Praise of God," *Ensign*, November 1975.

254 *The Brown-Driver-Briggs Hebrew and English Lexicon*, 210.

255 Elaine S. Dalton, "Remember Who You Are!" *Ensign*, May 2010.

256 *The Brown-Driver-Briggs Hebrew and English Lexicon*, 431.

257 Bible Dictionary, "Fear," 643.

258 David A. Bednar, "Therefore They Hushed Their Fears," *Ensign*, April 2015.

259 Camille Fronk Olson, *Women of the Old Testament* (Salt Lake City: Deseret Book, 2009), 179.

260 *John Gill's an Exposition of the Old Testament* (1697–1771) (Philadelphia: William W. Woodward, 1978), 6 v.; 28 cm., English. BYU Shaw-Shoemaker Microfiche Collection.

261 The actual verb used here is *Natan*, and the conjugation of *tenu* is the imperative verb form implying a command or request. *The Brown-Driver-Briggs Hebrew and English Lexicon*, 678.

262 *John Gill's An Exposition of the Old Testament* (1697–1771), Philadelphia: Printed by William W. Woodward, 1978, 6 v.; 28 cm., English. BYU Shaw-Shoemaker Microfiche Collection.

263 Dallin H. Oaks, "The Challenge to Become," *Ensign*, November 2000.

264 *Christ and the New Covenant*, 333–334.

265 Dieter F. Uchtdorf, "O How Great the Plan of Our God!" *Ensign*, November 2016.

266 Hugh Nibley, *Teachings of the Book of Mormon*, vol.4. (Salt Lake City: Deseret Book, 1993), 230. "He's going to give you the best you want. You're getting let off as easy as [possible]. You'd prefer hell a thousand times so that you won't have to [be in his presence], so that's what you get, if you want it. You know the kind of people you like, and you want to be with. Everyone's going to get the easiest possible sentence here. You'll be far 'more miserable to dwell with a holy and just God,' so they're not going to make you. You'll say thank heaven for that. God, you're being very kind, not making me dwell here. We're adjusted to what we're willing to take and what we're able to take. There's justice and mercy all the way here."

267 *The Brown-Driver-Briggs Hebrew and English Lexicon*, 237.

268 Hugh Nibley, *Temples and Cosmos: Beyond this Ignorant Present* (Salt Lake City: Deseret Book, 1992), 225. Wisdom of Solomon 3:5–7, The book of the Wisdom of Solomon is apocryphal. Written in praise of "Wisdom" and in condemnation of those who willfully rejected her, it purports to be addressed by the Israelite king Solomon to the kings and rulers of the earth. Many scholars feel it is of first century AD origin, in the Greek language. It shows traces of the influence of Greek philosophy. The most famous passages are those containing the description of "the righteous man" (4:7–18) and the picture of "Wisdom" (Wisdom 7–9). See "Apocrypha," LDS Bible Dictionary, 610.

269 Bruce R. McConkie, *Mormon Doctrine*, 640.

270 Guide to the Scriptures, "Elect," https://www.churchofjesuschrist. org/scriptures/gs/elect?lang=eng. Also, Joseph Smith said at the first Nauvoo Relief Society meeting that it also means elected— like Emma was elected to preside.

271 See Russell M. Nelson, "Children of the Covenant," *Ensign*, May 1995.

272 Stephen E. Robinson, H. Dean Garrett, *A Commentary on the Doctrine and Covenants* vol. 1, (Salt Lake City: Deseret Book, 2001), 173.

273 *Doctrine and Covenants and Church History Seminary Teacher Manual*, Lesson 154, Doctrine and Covenants 138:1–24; 38–50.

274 See Henry B. Eyring, "Daughters in the Covenant," *Ensign*, May 2014.

About the Author

TAMARA UZELAC HALL GREW UP in Utah and Missouri. She fully intended to get married and raise her twelve children while putting her husband through medical school . . . but God had other plans. She went to college and received both her bachelor's and master's degrees from BYU. She served a mission in Fresno, California. Then she worked as a social worker until God steered her life in a completely different direction and she became a full-time seminary and institute teacher. After buying a house and settling nicely into a family ward, she was set up on yet another blind date, this one with a widower, which miraculously worked out and catapulted her into married life and the role of an insta-mom to two little girls. Currently, she and her husband are the parents of four girls and live in Utah. She is a host for Time Out for Women and a featured speaker at Temple Square Youth Conferences, and she also speaks at Retreat for Girls, girls camps, and BYU Women's Conferences. She loves all things scriptural and is a lifelong student of the Hebrew language. A good flash mob makes her cry, she is a (self-proclaimed) champion Oreo eater, and she believes that cheese is God's way of saying, "Hey, everything is going to be okay."